Sola Scriptura!

The Protestant Position on the Bible

Dr. W. Robert Godfrey
Rev. James White
Dr. R.C. Sproul
Dr. John Armstrong
Dr. John Macarthur
Dr. Sinclair Ferguson
Dr. Joel Beeke
Rev. Ray Lanning

Rev. Don Kistler, General Editor

Soli Deo Gloria Publications
...for instruction in righteousness...

Soli Deo Gloria Publications
P.O. Box 451, Morgan, PA 15064
(412) 221-1901/FAX 221-1902

*

*

ISBN 1-57358-28-7

Contents

Author Profiles

Dr. W. Robert Godfrey is President of Westminster Theological Seminary in California in Escondido, California. He is also Professor of Church History. He received the A.B., M.A., and Ph.D. degrees from Stanford University, and the M.Div. degree from Gordon-Conwell Theological Seminary. He has taught at Westminster Theological Seminary (both in Pennsylvania and California) for over twenty years. He is an ordained minister in the Christian Reformed Church. Dr. Godfrey was a contributor to *John Calvin: His Influence on the Western World; Reformed Theology in America;* and *Scripture and Truth.* He edited the *Westminster Theological Journal* for several years, and is a frequent speaker at Christian conferences. Dr. Godfrey is a native of California. He and his wife Mary Ellen have three children: William, Mari, and Robert.

Rev. James White is Scholar-in-Residence in the College of Christian Studies at Grand Canyon University in Arizona and is Adjunct Professor teaching Greek for Golden Gate Baptist Theological Seminary. He holds a bachelor's degree in Bible and a minor in Biblical Greek from Grand Canyon

University, where he graduated *Summa Cum Laude*, and was a Ray Maben Scholar. He holds a master's degree in theology from Fuller Theological Seminary, Pasadena, California. An ordained Baptist minister, he is the author of seven books including *The Fatal Flaw, Answers to Catholic Claims, Justification by Faith, Letters to a Mormon Elder,* and *The King James Only Controversy.* As the director of Alpha and Omega Ministries, a Christian apologetics ministry based in Phoenix, James has engaged in numerous public debates against the leading Roman Catholic apologists across the nation on subjects such as *sola Scriptura,* the Mass, the Papacy, and justification by faith.

Dr. R.C. Sproul is founder and President of Ligonier Ministries of Orlando, Florida. He is a graduate of Westminster Theological Seminary in Philadelphia and holds a degree from the Free University of Amsterdam. A prolific author, he is an ordained minister in the Presbyterian Church of America. Dr. Sproul is in constant demand as a speaker and author. He has authored many books, among them *The Holiness of God; Chosen by God; Abortion: A Rational Look at an Emotional Issue;* and *Knowing Scripture.* Dr. Sproul was a contributing author to *Justification by Faith ALONE!,* previously published by Soli Deo Gloria.

Dr. John H. Armstrong is Director of Reformation & Revival Ministries, Inc., Carol Stream, Illinois. He is editor of the Reformation & Revival Journal, an itinerant preacher and lecturer, and author of *Can Fallen Pastors Be Restored?* (Moody Press, 1995) and *A View of Rome* (Moody Press, 1995). He edited *Roman Catholicism: Evangelical Protestants Analyze What Unites & Divides Us* (Moody Press, 1994) and *The Coming Evangelical Crisis: Modern Challenges to the Authority of Scripture & the Gospel* (1996). He has contributed to numerous journals and magazines including *Christianity Today, Trinity Journal* and *The Standard,* and was a contributor to *Justification by Faith ALONE!.*

Dr. John MacArthur is pastor/teacher at Grace Community Church in Sun Valley, California. A graduate of Talbot Theological Seminary, he can be heard daily throughout the country on his radio program "Grace To You." He is the author of numerous bestsellers, among them *The Gospel According to Jesus, The Vanishing Conscience, Faith Works, Charismatic Chaos,* and his new book on discernment, *Reckless Faith.* Dr. MacArthur also serves as President of the Master's College and Seminary in Southern California. He was also a contributing author to *Justification by Faith ALONE!*

Dr. Sinclair Ferguson is Professor of Systematic Theology at Westminster Theological Seminary in Philadelphia. He is a graduate of the University of Aberdeen in Scotland, and holds both the M.A. and Ph.D. degrees from that institution. Since 1976 he has been assistant editor of the Banner of Truth Trust. Dr. Ferguson is the author of numerous books, among them *Taking the Christian Life Seriously, Know Your Christian Life, Grow in Grace, Discovering God's Will, A Heart for God, Kingdom Life in a Fallen World,* and *Handle with Care.* Dr. Ferguson is ordained in the Church of Scotland and maintains a worldwide ministry, preaching and teaching in churches and conferences. He and his wife Dorothy have four children.

Dr. Joel R. Beeke is the pastor of the Heritage Netherlands Reformed Congregation in Grand Rapids, Michigan; President and Professor of Systematic Theology at Puritan Reformed Theological Seminary; editor of the *Banner of Sovereign Grace Truth;* President of Reformation Heritage Books; President of Inheritance Publishers; Vice-President of the Dutch Reformed Translation Society; and radio pastor to Europe and Latin America. He earned a Ph.D. in Reformation and Post-Reformation Theology from Westminster Theological Seminary in Philadelphia, where he has also lectured and serves as an adjunct professor of theology. He is the author of *Assurance of Faith: Calvin, English Puritanism, and The Dutch Second Reformation,* as well as of several other books and numerous articles. He is frequently called upon to lecture at seminaries and to speak at Reformed conferences in North America and around the world. He and his wife, Mary, have two children, Calvin and Esther, and are expecting a third. Dr. Beeke was a contributing author to *Justification by Faith ALONE!*

Rev. Ray B. Lanning is pastor of the Independent Reformed Church of Cutlerville in Grand Rapids, Michigan. He is a graduate of Westminster Theological Seminary and has done graduate work at Calvin Theological Seminary. Ordained to the ministry in 1977, he has served Presbyterian and Reformed churches in various parts of the U.S. and Canada. He and his wife, Linda, have four children.

Preface

Christianity is based upon revelation. If God in all His sovereign majesty did not choose to reveal Himself to mankind, there would be no true knowledge of Him nor the possibility of a true relationship with Him. We are bound to Him by what He has chosen to reveal to us about Himself. All the efforts to get to know God by man-created means lead to false religions or mysticisms. Consequently, the primary question governing our relationship with God is the question of submission— either to His revelation or to our imagination. The former requires that we rely upon a divine influence over our minds, which must be submissive to the truth of the Revealer. The latter depends upon the amassing of propositions, theses, and traditions: a mixture of philosophy, psychology, and theology—a man-made "philo-psycho-theology." In this atmosphere, the words of the revelation of God no longer have the meanings designated them by the Holy Spirit, but rather affirm the mysteries of the religions or idolatries man has created.

The historical Protestant doctrine of *sola Scriptura*—Scripture alone—affirms that God has an eternal plan to make known the mysteries of the gospel which He wishes to be known by us. Thus, Protestant theology (doctrines about God) flows from the act of divine will by which He wishes to make known truth to us, which is accomplished by His words or His works as revealed in Christ. "No man has seen God at any time; the only begotten Son, which is in the bosom of the Father, He has declared Him" (John 1:18). The revelation of the divine mind and will which we have in *sola Scriptura* is dependent upon revelation from God Himself. It is an example of God's merciful kindness to fallen humanity that He has willed that all of the knowledge needful for a relationship *with* Him, and for correct worship *of* Him, should be provided *by* Him. If it were not so, we would stumble in our own blindness. It is to the revelation of the divine mind expressed in *sola Scriptura* that all of our thoughts and doctrine, our worship of Him and our obedience to Him, must always be conformed.

It is for this reason that Soli Deo Gloria has published this work. The spirit of our age would have the Church disregard this issue for the sake of unity. Biblical unity must be based upon biblical truth, not human intentions. The example of unity we have in Scripture is the Trinity, which is in complete agreement on everything! Too often what passes for unity is really compromise. It is better to be divided by truth than united in error.

It is also because of our love for the Church that we produce this book. Love, true love, cannot be divorced from truth. Scripture is quite clear that love rejoices in the truth! One cannot claim to love when one is not concerned about truth. The truth of Scripture must be the concern of one who truly loves. In an age where the absolute authority of the Scripture has been jettisoned for the sake of agreement at the expense of doctrinal distinctives, we must be reminded that for real unity to exist among Christians, it must be based upon the unadulterated truth of the Gospel of Jesus Christ contained in the Scriptures alone.

A conscience that is bound by the Word of God is a force that no nation, system, or age can withstand. It is the desire of Soli Deo Gloria to call God's people back to a position of power—the power of *sola Scriptura.*

Dr. Bruce Bickel
Chairman of the Board of Directors
Soli Deo Gloria

Mr. John Bishop   Rev. Don Kistler
Annapolis, MD   *Pittsburgh, PA*
Mr. Peter Neumeier   Rev. Lance Quinn
Atlanta, GA   *Sun Valley, CA*

Foreword

It was a time of prosperity and ease, with peace on the often-troubled borders, as the surrounding nations that had built threatening empires fell into internal decay and lethargy. Attracted by the idols of the nations, God's people again fell into false worship, and this "truth decay" led to incredible depths of social injustice and immorality. Although the churches were full and, according to the reports, the worship was lively, God was not pleased. Nearly 800 years before Christ's birth, Amos—a "jack of all trades" (shepherd, fig tree dresser, and livestock breeder)—was called by God to look after the spiritual flock whose self-satisfied condition had occasioned apostasy. " 'Behold, the days are coming,' says the Lord GOD, 'that I will send a famine on the land, not a famine of bread, nor a thirst for water, but of hearing the words of the LORD. They shall wander from sea to sea, and from north to east; they shall run to and fro, seeking the word of the LORD, but shall not find it' " (Amos 8:11–12).

God's Word had been the center of Israel's life, as it had been ever since Creation itself:

"And God said, 'Let there be light!' " It is God's
own utterance that creates the universe and pre-
serves it through history. It is His Word that
promised blessing to Adam and his posterity for
obedience, and warned of a curse for breaking
the solemn covenant. That same word announced judgment for transgression and then
justification by the Messiah who is to come.
Through faith in the One promised through this
Word from above, the damned could be re-
deemed and reconciled to God. The direct expression of His own character and will, God's
Word was incapable of being distinguished—
much less divorced—from God Himself. His
people never conceived of such utterances as the
mere reflections of humanity in its spiritual
quest, but never knew that God's speech was
equivalent to His person. His Word, both in
command and promise, was not only to have
the last word, but the first word and every word
in between, in all matters concerning doctrine
and the Christian life.

However, we fallen sinners are creative folk.
We do not appreciate being told from above
what to believe and how to conduct ourselves in
this life. "I Did It My Way" expressed the sentiment of the rebellious human heart. Israel
sought to worship God in its own way, in a

manner that accommodated the felt needs of worshipers. Other "words" were added, leading the people away from the clear and simple teaching of Scripture, and even though this path always led to divine judgment in earthly exiles, the people never seemed to learn their lessons about adding to Scripture (legalism) or subtracting from it (antinomianism). But God's Word is what it is, whether we acknowledge it or not. If we do not accept it, God's Word judges us anyway. If we do, it announces its saving promise of eternal life in Christ. Throughout the prophetic literature, we notice a common theme: the false prophets tell the people what they want to hear, baptize it with God's name, and serve it up as God's latest word to His people.

As it was in the days of the judges, the kings, and the prophets, so it is in our day: There is a famine in the land for God's Word. False prophets abound promising "peace, peace, when there is no peace," as the shepherd is replaced by the rancher and the pastor with the manager-therapist-coach-entertainer.

Like Israel, wanting to experience God on her own terms, the medieval church preferred idolatry to true worship and relied on visual forms created by the human imagination when she should have been sustained by the written and preached Word. In our own day, we too find ourselves immersed in a visual culture where words in general are both unimportant and viewed with a growing cynicism. Reflecting the contemporary attitude in both the academy and popular culture, a pop group sings, "What are words for?"

And yet, Christianity is a religion of words, a religion of the Book. Like the Reformers, we too must not accommodate to a visually or experientially oriented culture in the interest of marketing success, but must pour all of our energies into a word-centered community, however out of step with contemporary society that may be. The Reformers insisted that Scripture not only has the final say, but it is the *formal* principle of everything we believe about doctrine or conduct. That is, it shapes and forms our faith. It does not simply sign off on essentially secular definitions of reality borrowed from psychology, business, sociology, politics, and the like. Rather, it is more likely to overthrow our presuppositions. Here, the Reformers distinguished between "things heavenly" and "things earthly." In the latter realm, including science, art, and philosophy, unbelievers could contribute to the advance of knowledge and experience. After all, Scripture is not interested in telling us everything about everything, and God's world is open to the investigation of everyone. But the transcendent realities of God's character, His commands and His saving work, are not available to the philosopher, scientist, artist, or therapist. Secular wisdom may lead us to the truth about the revolution of planets, but it cannot explain the nature of God, the self and guilt and redemption. It cannot lead us to the truth about how we are saved from God's wrath, for it refuses to believe that this is even a reality in the first place. "The preaching of the cross is foolishness to those who are perishing," said the Apostle Paul, because it does not fit the questions—much less the answers—of secular wisdom.

But in our day preaching cannot be foolish. It must be "relevant," which is the word we have drafted into the service of market-driven approaches. In contrast, the message of the cross assumes the terror of the Law, divine wrath towards sinners (and not just their sins), and the need for a substitutionary sacrifice to assuage divine justice. It assumes that the greatest problem facing humanity is original and actual sin—personal rebellion against a holy God—not stress, low self-esteem, and a failure to realize one's full potential.

With all of these challenges—a visually ori-

ented and consumer-driven society—there has
arisen another famine of God's Word in the
land. His Law, consisting of all the Bible's
commands and threats for violating divine holiness, has been reduced to helpful principles for
personal well-being, so that one may feel unsat-
isfied, but not condemned. His gospel, consisting of all the Bible's promises of salvation for
sinners through Christ's perfect life, death, resurrection, and saving offices, has been similarly
reduced to platitudes. In short, God's Word has
been replaced with human words, not only in
mainline churches, but within the mainstream
evangelical movement as well. We have forgot-
ten, it seems, that the Word creates life and that
it is the source of the church's growth and maturity.

Not only must we recover the official commitment to the sufficiency of Scripture, it must
be the *only* voice we hear from those who assume the momentous task of being God's
spokesmen. And God's spokesmen must ring
the bells on this point. While this book has the
Roman Church's view of Scripture in mind
when it asserts Protestantism's position, it is
Protestantism that this book is trying to reach as
much as Rome! This book laments that Rome is
so aggressive with its error, yes, but equally that

Protestantism is so passive in its capitulation! It is not just that the walls of the city are being assaulted, but the Protestant Church seems to have thrown the key to the city out to the invaders!

But this book is not simply a lamentation; it is a way forward. Here is the Protestant position majestically stated; here is the Scripture exalted. This book attempts to assess the present situation with a view to calling the shepherds of Israel to hear God's voice again and make it plain to a new generation. Fulfilled already in Christ, may the prophecy of Amos receive fresh relevance in our own day: " 'On that day I will raise up the tabernacle of David, which has fallen down, and repair its damages; I will raise up its ruins, and rebuild as in the days of old; that they may possess the remnant of Edom, and all the Gentiles who are called by My name,' says the LORD who does this thing" (Amos 9:11–12). Let us pray to the Lord of the harvest for relief from this famine and for spiritual plenty in the years to come!

Michael Horton
December 1995

1

What Do We Mean by *Sola Scriptura*?

by Dr. W. Robert Godfrey

There are two main issues that divide Protestant Catholics from Roman Catholics. Both groups claim to be catholic, that is, part of the apostolic, universal church of Jesus Christ. Roman Catholics believe we Protestants departed from that church in the sixteenth century. Protestant Catholics believe they departed earlier.

The theme of this opening chapter is one of the issues that still divides us: the source of religious truth for the people of God. (The other main issue, that of how a man is made right with God, has been dealt with in the book *Justification by Faith ALONE!*, published by Soli Deo Gloria in 1995.) As Protestants we maintain that the Scripture alone is our authority. Our Roman opponents maintain that the Scripture by itself is insufficient as the authority of the people of God, and that tradition and the teaching authority of the church must be added to the Scripture.

This is a solemn topic. This is no time for games. We must be searching for the truth. God has declared that whoever adds to or takes away from His Word is subject to His curse. The Roman church has declared that we Protestants are accursed ("anathematized") for taking away the Word of God as found in tradition. We Protestants have declared that the Roman church is a false church for adding human traditions to the Word of God. Despite sincere debates by fine apologists over the course of nearly 500 years, the differences remain basically as they were in the sixteenth century. I will not say much new here, but we must continue to pursue the truth.

In spite of the difficulty of this undertaking, I am eager to join that historic train of Protestant apologists to defend the doctrine that the Scripture alone is our ultimate religious authority. I believe that it can be shown that this position is the clear position of Scripture itself. And I hope that, by the grace of God, those committed to the Roman doctrine of tradition will come to see the tragic error of denigrating the sufficiency and perspicuity of God's own inspired Word.

Let me begin with certain clarifications so as not to be misunderstood. I am not arguing that all truth is to be found in the Bible, or that the Bible is the only form in which the truth of God has come to His people. I am not arguing that every verse in the Bible is equally clear to every reader. Nor am I arguing that the church—both the people of God and the ministerial office—is not of great value and help in understanding the Scripture. As William Whitaker stated in his noble work: "For we also say that the church is the interpreter of Scripture, and that the gift of interpretation resides only in the church: but we deny that it pertains to particular persons, or is tied to any particular see or succession of men."[1]

The Protestant position, and my position, is that all things *necessary* for salvation and concerning faith and life are taught in the Bible clearly enough for the ordinary believer to find it there and understand.

The position I am defending certainly is what is taught in the Bible itself. For example, Deuteronomy 31:9 states: "Moses wrote down this law. . . ." Moses instructed the people by writing down the law and then ordering that it be read to them "so they can listen and learn to fear the Lord your God and follow carefully all the words of this law," Deuteronomy 31:9, 12.

Moses declared to all Israel: "Take to heart all the words I have solemnly declared to you this day, so that you may command your children to obey carefully all the words of this law. They are not just idle words for you, they are your life," Deuteronomy 32:46–47.

Notice the clear elements in these passages:

1. The Word of which Moses spoke was written.
2. The people can and must listen to it and learn it.
3. In this Word they can find life.

The people do not need any additional institution to interpret the Word. The priests, prophets, and scribes of Israel certainly function to help the people ministerially. But the Word alone was sufficient for salvation. The prophets, who were indeed inspired, came very much in the spirit of Micah who said, "He has shown you, O man, what is good," Micah 6:8. The function of the prophets and priests was not to add to or even clarify the law; rather, they applied it to the people who were sinfully indifferent

If this principle of the sufficiency and clarity of the Word is true in the Old Testament, we can assume that it is all the more true in the New. The New Testament gloriously fulfills what the Old Testament promises. But we do not have to assume it; rather, the New Testament makes clear that the character of Scripture is to be sufficient and clear. One example of that is found in 2 Timothy 3–4. Here Paul writes to his younger brother in the faith, Timothy. He writes that Timothy—who was instructed in the faith by his mother and grandmother—has also learned all about Paul's teaching (3:10). Timothy has been mightily helped by all sorts of oral teaching, some of it apostolic. Yet Paul writes these words to Timothy:

> And indeed, all who desire to live godly in Christ Jesus will be persecuted. But evil men and impostors will proceed from bad to worse, deceiving and being deceived. You, however, continue in the things you have learned and become convinced of, knowing from whom you have learned them; and that from childhood you have known the sacred writings which are able to give you the wisdom that leads to salvation through faith which is in Christ Jesus. All Scripture is inspired by God and profitable for teaching, for reproof, for correction, for training in righteousness; that the man of God may be adequate, equipped for every good work. I solemnly charge you in the presence of God and of Christ Jesus, who is to judge the living and the dead, and

by His appearing and His kingdom: preach
the word; be ready in season and out of
season; reprove, rebuke, exhort, with great
patience and instruction. For the time will
come when they will not endure sound
doctrine; but wanting to have their ears
tickled, they will accumulate for themselves
teachers in accordance to their own desires;
and will turn away their ears from the
truth, and will turn aside to myths. But
you, be sober in all things, endure hard-
ship, do the work of an evangelist, fulfill
your ministry. (2 Timothy 3:12–4:5)

You see, Paul reminds Timothy that the
Scriptures are able to make him wise unto salvation in Christ Jesus (3:15). He teaches that the
Scriptures are useful for teaching, reproof
(rebuking), correcting, and training in righteousness (3:16). Because the Scriptures have this
character, they thoroughly equip the man of God
for every good work (3:17). So Paul tells Timothy
that he must preach this Word, even though the
time is coming when people will not want to
hear it, but rather will want teachers to suit their
fancy, who will instruct them in myths rather
than the truth of the Word (4:1–4).

The force and clarity of the Apostle's teaching
here are striking. In spite of the rich oral
teaching Timothy had, he is to preach the

Scriptures because those Scriptures give him clearly all that he needs for wisdom and preparation to instruct the people of God in faith and all good works. The Scripture makes him wise for salvation, and equips him with everything he needs for doing every good work required of the preacher of God. The sufficiency and clarity of the Word are taught in this one section of Scripture over and over again. John Chrysostom paraphrased the meaning of Paul's words to Timothy this way: "You have Scripture for a master instead of me; from there you can learn whatever you would know."[2]

I have listened to several taped debates on this topic. Often Protestant apologists have cited 2 Timothy 3 against Roman opponents. The usual response of Catholic apologists is to repeatedly assert that 2 Timothy 3 does not teach sufficiency. Sometimes they will refer to James 1:4, Matthew 19:21, or Colossians 1:28 and 4:12 as parallel texts, claiming that the word "complete" in 2 Timothy 3:17 does not mean sufficient. But such passages are not parallel; a completely different Greek word is used. Where 2 Timothy 3:17 uses *exartizo,* which has to do with being fitted for a task, these other passages use the Greek word *teleios*, which has reference to maturity or having reached a desired end.

Repeated assertions do not prove a point; that is only a propaganda technique. Our opponents need to answer in a responsible, thorough way.

The confidence that Paul had in the Scriptures, and which he taught Timothy, was clearly understood by the great church father, Augustine. In his treatise to prepare leaders of the church in an understanding of the Bible (*On Christian Doctrine*), Augustine wrote: "Among those things which are said openly in Scripture are to be found all those teachings which involve faith, the mores of living, and that hope and charity which we have discussed."[3]

We should not be surprised that the Apostle Paul, the Old Testament, and the greatest teacher of the ancient church held to the sufficiency and perspicuity of Scripture. It is the position that Jesus took in one of the most important moments of his life. At the beginning of his public ministry, Jesus faced the focused temptation of the devil in the wilderness. He faced the temptation as the Son of God, but also as the second Adam and the true Israel. And how did He face that temptation? He did not appeal to the oral tradition of Israel; He did not appeal to the authority of the rabbis or Sanhedrin; He did not even appeal to His own divinity or the inspiration of the Holy Spirit. Our Savior, in the face of temptation, turned again and again and again to the Scriptures. "It is written," He said.

The Scriptures made Him wise; they equipped Him for every good work. They were clear, as He implied that even the evil one knew. When the devil quoted the Scripture, Jesus did not turn to some other authority. Rather Jesus said, "It is also written."

When the evil one or his representatives misuse the Bible, or imply that it is unclear, Jesus teaches us that we must look more deeply into the written Word, not away from it.

Roman apologists will attempt to convince us that these texts of Scripture do not mean what they clearly say. Let me anticipate some of their arguments and prepare you for some of the ways they tend to respond.

1. The Word of God. First, they will try to say that the phrase "the Word of God" can mean more than just the Bible. I have already granted that. The question before us is whether *today* anything other than the Scriptures is necessary to know the truth of God for salvation. The Scripture texts I have cited show that nothing else is needed. Our opponents need to show not that Paul referred to his preaching as well as his writing as the Word of God—I grant that; they need to show that Paul taught that the oral

teaching of the apostles would be needed to supplement the Scriptures for the Church through the ages. They cannot show that because Paul did not *teach* that, and the Scriptures *as a whole* do not teach that!

2. Tradition. Our Roman opponents, while making much of tradition, will never really define tradition or tell you what its content is. Tradition is a word that can be used in a variety of ways. It can refer to a certain school of understanding the Scriptures, such as the Lutheran tradition. It can refer to traditions—supposedly from the apostles—that are not in the Bible. It can refer to developing traditions in the history of the church that are clearly not ancient in origin. Usually, in the ancient fathers of the church, the word "tradition" refers to the standard interpretation of the Bible among them. And we Protestants value such traditions.

But what do Roman apologists mean when they assert the authority of tradition? Historically, they have not agreed among themselves about the nature and content of tradition. For example, one has said that tradition does not add anything to Scripture. But almost all Roman apologists, for over three hundred years after the Council of Trent, argued that tradition *does* add to the Scriptures. Some Roman apologists believe that all binding tradition was taught by the apostles, while others believe that tradition evolves and develops through the centuries of the church so that there are traditions necessary for salvation that were never known to the apostles. It is impossible to know what the real Roman position is on this matter.

The Second Vatican Council expressed itself with deliberate ambiguity: "This tradition which comes from the apostles develops in the Church with the help of the Holy Spirit. For there is a growth in the understanding of the realities and the words which have been handed down. . . . For as the centuries succeed one another, the Church constantly moves forward toward the fulness of divine truth until the words of God reach their complete fulfillment in her."[4] What does that mean? It certainly does not give us any clear understanding of the character or content of tradition.

Rome usually tries to clarify its position by saying that its authority is Scripture, tradition, and church together. Vatican II declared: "It is clear, therefore, that sacred tradition, sacred Scripture, and the teaching authority of the Church, in accord with God's most wise design, are so linked and joined together that one cannot stand without the others, and that all together and each in its own way under the action of the one Holy Spirit contribute effectively to the salvation of souls."[5]

In fact, however, if you listen carefully, you will notice that the real authority for Rome is neither Scripture *nor* tradition, but the church. What is the Scripture, and what does it teach? Only the church can tell you. What is tradition, and what does it teach? Only the church can tell you. As the Roman theologian John Eck said, "The Scriptures are not authentic, except by the authority of the church."[6] As Pope Pius IX said at the time of the First Vatican Council in 1870, "I am tradition."[7] The overwhelming arrogance of such a statement is staggering. But it confirms our claim that, for Rome, the only real authority is the church: *sola ecclesia.*

Now Protestantism arose in the sixteenth century in reaction to such claims and teachings of the Roman church. In the Middle Ages, most within the church had believed that the Bible and the tradition of the church taught the same, or at least complementary, doctrines. But as Luther and others studied the Bible with a greater care and depth than the church had done in centuries, they began to discover that tradition actually contradicted the Bible. They discovered that, for example:

(1) The Bible teaches that the office of bishop and presbyter are the same office (Titus 1:5–7), but tradition says they are different offices.

(2) The Bible teaches that all have sinned except Jesus (Romans 3:10–12, Hebrews 4:15), but tradition says that Mary was sinless.

(3) The Bible teaches that Christ offered His sacrifice once for all (Hebrews 7:27, 9:28, 10:10), but tradition says that the priest sacrifices Christ on the altar at mass.

(4) The Bible says that we are not to bow down to statues (Exodus 20:4–5), but tradition says that we should bow down to statues.

(5) The Bible says that all Christians are saints and priests (Ephesians 1:1; 1 Peter 2:9), but tradition says that saints and priests are special castes within the Christian community.

(6) The Bible says that Jesus is the only Mediator between God and man (1 Timothy 2:5), but tradition says Mary is co-mediator with Christ.

(7) The Bible says that all Christians should know that they have eternal life (1 John 5:13), but tradition says that all Christians cannot and should not know that they have eternal life.

The Reformers saw that the words of Jesus to the Pharisees applied equally to their day: "You nullify the Word of God for the sake of your tradition" (Matthew 15:6).

The Reformers also discovered that tradition contradicted tradition. For example, the tradition of the Roman church teaches that the pope is the head of the church, a bishop over all bishops. But Gregory the Great, pope and saint at the end of the ancient church period, said that such a teaching came from the spirit of Antichrist ("I confidently affirm that whosoever calls himself *sacerdos universalis,* or desires to be so called by others is in his pride a forerunner of Antichrist").[8]

More directly related to our discussion is the evident tension in tradition about the value of reading the Bible. *The Index of Forbidden Books* of Pope Pius IV in 1559 said:

> Since experience teaches that, if the reading of the Holy Bible in the vernacular is permitted generally without discrimination, more damage than advantage will result because of the boldness of men, the judgment of the bishops and inquisitors is to serve as guide in this regard. Bishops and inquisitors may, in accord with the counsel of the local priest and confessor, allow Catholic translations of the Bible to be read by those of whom they realize that such reading will not lead to the detriment but to the increase of faith and piety. The permission is to be given in writing. Whoever reads or

has such a translation in his possession
without this permission cannot be ab-
solved from his sins until he has turned in
these Bibles.[9]

In marked contrast, Vatican II stated: "Easy
access to sacred Scripture should be provided
for all the Christian faithful. . . . Since the word of
God should be available at all times, the Church
with maternal concern sees to it that suitable
and correct translations are made into different
languages, especially from the original texts of
the sacred books."[10] Does tradition believe that
the Bible is dangerous or helpful? The Bible did
prove dangerous in the sixteenth century; most
who read it carefully became Protestants!

Such discoveries about tradition led the
Reformers back to the Bible. There they learned
that the Scriptures must stand as judge of all
teaching. The Scripture teaches that it is the revelation of God, and is therefore true in all that it
teaches. But nowhere does the Scripture say that
the church is true in all it says. Rather, although
the church as a whole will be preserved in the
faith, wolves will arise in the church (Acts
20:29–30), and even the man of lawlessness will
sit at the heart of the church teaching lies (2
Thessalonians 2:4).

3. This brings us to our third concern, the

church and the canon. Our Roman opponents
will use the word "church" repeatedly. Those of
us who are Protestants will normally be inclined
to interpret their use of the word "church" as referring to the body of the faithful. But that is not
the way they characteristically use the word.
When they refer to the authority of the church,
they mean the infallible teaching authority of
councils and popes. That view of the church
they take from the Middle Ages and in a roman-
tic way read back into the ancient church period. So notice very carefully how they use the
word "church." And remember that neither the
Scriptures, nor the great majority of the fathers
of the ancient church period, understand the authority of the church in the way they do.

     Let me offer as an illustration two examples
from the work of Augustine, often quoted
against the Protestant position on the question
of the authority of the church. At one point in
his debate with the Pelagians, a bishop of Rome
sided with Augustine, and Augustine declared,
"Rome has spoken, the matter is settled." Later,
however, another pope opposed Augustine on
this subject, and Augustine responded by saying, "Christ has spoken, the matter is settled."
Augustine did not bow to the authority of the
bishop of Rome, but turned to the word of Christ

to evaluate the teaching of Rome.

Another statement of Augustine's, often cited by Roman apologists, reads: "I would not have believed had not the authority of the catholic church moved me." That seems very strong and clear. But in another place Augustine wrote: "I would never have understood Plotinus had not the authority of my neo-Platonic teachers moved me." This parallel shows that Augustine is not talking about some absolute, infallible authority in the church, but rather about the ministerial work of the church and about teachers who help students understand.

Let us look at the church further by raising a related issue: the canon of Scripture. Romanists will try to make much of the issue of the canon. They will tell you that the Bible alone cannot be our authority because the Bible does not tell us what books are in the Bible. They will argue that the church must tell us what books are in the Bible. When they say the church tells us, they mean popes and councils must tell us. This implies that we did not have a Bible until Pope Damasus offered a list of the canon in 382, or, perhaps, until 1546 when the Council of Trent became the first "ecumenical" council to define the canon. But of course the people of God had the Bible before 1546 and before 382.

In the first place, the church always had Scripture. The apostolic preaching and writing of the first century repeatedly verified its teaching by quoting from the Old Testament. The quotations from, and allusions to, the Old Testament abound in the New Testament. The New Testament does not reject the Old, but fulfills it (Romans 1:2; Luke 16:29; Ephesians 2:19–20). The church always had a canonical foundation in the Old Testament.

In the second place, we can see that the apostles sensed that the new covenant inaugurated by our Lord Jesus would have a new or augmented canon. Canon and covenant are interrelated and interdependent in the Bible (see Meredith G. Kline, *The Structure of Biblical Authority*). Peter testifies to this emerging canon when he includes the letters of Paul as part of the Scriptures (2 Peter 3:16).

In the third place, we must see that the canon of Scripture is, in a real sense, established by the Scripture itself, because the canonical books are self-authenticating. As God's revelation, they are recognized by the people of God as God's own Word. As Jesus said, "I am the good shepherd; I know My sheep and My sheep know Me. They . . . will listen to My voice" (John 10:14–16). In the deepest sense we cannot judge the Word, but the Word judges us. "For the word of God is living and active. Sharper than any double-edged sword, it penetrates even to dividing of soul and spirit, joints and marrow; it judges the thoughts and attitudes of the heart" (Hebrews 4:12). The self-authenticating character of the canon is demonstrated by the remarkable unanimity reached by the people of God on the canon.

In the fourth place, we must see that historically the canon was formed not by popes and councils; these actions simply recognized the emerging consensus of the people of God as they recognized the authentic Scriptures. Indeed, whatever criteria were used by popes and councils to recognize the canon (authorship, style, content, witness of the Spirit, etc.), these same criteria were available to the people of God as a whole.

We can see this basic understanding of the formation of the canon stated in *The New Catholic Encyclopedia* which states: "The canon, already implicitly present in the apostolic age, gradually became explicit through a number of providential factors forming and fixing it."[11]

We can also see this basic approach to the canon reflected in the words of Augustine, writing in his important treatise entitled *On Chris-*

tian Doctrine. This treatise was written between 396 and 427—after the supposedly authoritative decision of Pope Damasus on the canon, and after a council held in Hippo had discussed the canon. Augustine wrote:

> In the matter of canonical Scriptures he should follow the authority of the greater number of catholic Churches, among which are those which have deserved to have apostolic seats and receive epistles. He will observe this rule concerning canonical Scriptures, that he will prefer those accepted by all catholic Churches to those which some do not accept; among those which are not accepted by all, he should prefer those which are accepted by the largest number of important Churches to those held by a few minor Churches of less authority. If he discovers that some are maintained by the larger number of Churches, others by the Churches of weightiest authority, although this condition is not likely, he should hold them to be of equal value.[12]

This statement shows that Augustine did not look to popes or councils for the solution of the question of the canon. He recognized the variety among churches, and the appropriateness of a plurality of churches. He urged all students of

Scripture to examine the question and to look for the emerging consensus among the people of God. Like Augustine, we do not disparage the value of the witness of the people of God to the canon. We value the ministry of the church in this as in all things. But we deny that the church in its offices or councils authoritatively establishes the Scripture on the basis of some knowledge or power not available to Christians generally. The character of the canonical books draws the people of God to them.

4. Unity. Notice how Catholics use the word "unity." They will suggest that we Protestants disprove our claim of the clarity of the Scripture by our failure to agree about the meaning of the Scripture. We recognize that Protestants are divided into various denominations. But all Protestants who are heirs of the Reformation are united in understanding the gospel and in respecting one another as brothers in Christ. We have all found the same gospel clearly in the Bible.

When we discuss unity and authority, let us be certain that we are making fair and accurate comparisons. Our Roman opponents will want to compare Roman theory with Protestant practices. That is not fair. We must compare theory with theory or practice with practice. In practice, *neither* group has the agreement we should have.

Remember that while Rome is united organizationally, it is just as divided theologically as is Protestantism broadly understood. The institution of an infallible pope has not created theological unity in the Roman church. Rather, Roman theologians are constantly disagreeing with each other as to what the popes have taught, and as to whether those teachings are in fact proclaimed *ex cathedra,* and are therefore infallible. The modern state of the Roman church really has shown that the institution of the papacy has not made clear the necessary content of Christian truth. I suspect that every honest member of the Roman church will have to acknowledge that.

As early as the seventeenth century the Reformed theologian Francis Turretin noted the serious theological divisions in the Roman church and asked why the pope did not settle these disputes if his office was so effective.13 Such theological problems are certainly much greater today than in Turretin's day and the question remains unanswered as to why the pope is so ineffective.13

We should not be surprised that there are divisions in the church. Christ and His apostles predicted that there would be. The Apostle Paul told us that such divisions are useful. He wrote: "No doubt there have to be differences among you to show which of you have God's approval" (1 Corinthians 11:19). Differences should humble us and drive us back to the Scriptures to test all claims to truth. If we do not accept the Scriptures as our standard and judge, there is indeed no hope for unity.

The church must have a standard by which to judge all claims to truth. The church must have a standard of truth by which to reform and purify itself when divisions arise. The church cannot claim that it is that standard and defend that claim by appealing to itself. Such circular reasoning is not only unconvincing; it is self-defeating. Rome's argument boils down to this: we must believe Rome because Rome says so.

The Bible tells us that the Word of God is the light that enables us to walk in the ways of God. Listen to Psalm 119:99, 100, 105, 130: "I have more insight than all my teachers, for I meditate on Thy statutes. I have more understanding than the elders, for I obey Thy precepts. Thy word is a lamp unto my feet and a light for my path. The unfolding of Thy words gives light; it gives understanding to the simple."

Roman opponents usually object to an appeal to Psalm 119 on the grounds that it speaks

of the Word of God, not of the Bible, and therefore could include in its praise tradition as well
as Scripture. But their argument is irrelevant to
our use of Psalm 119, because we are using it to
prove the clarity, not the sufficiency of Scripture!
The Psalmist is saying here that the light of the
Word shines so brightly and clearly that if I
meditate on it and obey it, I am wiser than any
teacher or elder. The simple can understand it.
The Word is like a strong flashlight in a dark
forest. It enables me to walk on the path without
tripping.

We must listen to the Scriptures so that we
will act as God's Word teaches us to act.
Consider the story of Paul in Berea, Acts 17:10–
12. Paul preached there in the synagogue and
many Jews responded to his preaching with eagerness. We are told that after they listened to
Paul each day they examined the Scriptures to
see if what Paul said was true. How did Paul re-
act? Did he say that the Scriptures were not
clear, and that only he as an apostle or the rabbis or the Sanhedrin could tell them what the
Scriptures really meant? Or did he say that they
should not expect to find the truth in the
Scriptures because they were incomplete and
needed to be supplemented by tradition? Or did
he say that they were insulting his apostolic au-

thority, and that they should simply submit to him as the infallible interpreter of the Bible? Or did Paul say that they should defer to Peter as the only one who could interpret the Bible? No! He did not say any of these things. The practice of the Bereans is praised in the Bible. They are called noble because they evaluated everything on the basis of the written Word of God.

If we would be faithful children of God, if we would be noble, we must proceed as the Bereans did. We must follow the example of Moses and Paul and our Lord Jesus. Do not rest your confidence on the wisdom of men who claim infallibility. Stand rather with the Apostle Paul who wrote in 1 Corinthians 4:6, "Do not go beyond what is written."

---

1 William Whitaker, A Disputation on Holy Scripture (Cambridge,: University Press, 1849) p. 411.

2 Cited in Whitaker, p. 637.

3 Augustine, On Christian Doctrine trans. by D.W. Roberston, Jr. (New York: Liberal Arts Press, 1958) II:9.

4 The Documents of Vatican II, ed. Walter M. Abbott (New York: Herden and Herden, 1966) p. 116. Dei Verbum, 8.

5 Ibid., p. 118.

[6] John Eck, *Enchiridion of Commonplaces,* trans. by Ford Lewis Battles, (Grand Rapids: Baker, 1979) p. 13.

[7] Jesef Rupert Geiselmann, *The Meaning of Tradition* (Montreal: Palm Publishers, 1966) p. 16, note on pp. 113–114.

[8] Cited in *Cambridge Medieval History,* section written by W. H. Hutton, edited by H. M. Gwatkin and J. P. Whitney,(New York: The MacMillan Co., 1967) II:247.

[9] James Townley, *Illustrations of Biblical Literature,* Vol. 2 (London: printed for Longman, Hurst, Rees, Orme, and Brown, 1821) p. 481

[10] *Documents of Vatican II,* pp. 125–126.

[11] Cited in a tape by William Webster entitled "The Canon," available from Christian Resources, 304 West T Street, Battleground, WA 98604. This tape is part 3 of a 16 tape series entitled *Roman Catholic Tradition: Its Roots and Evolution.*

[12] *On Christian Doctrine,* Book 2 section VIII, trans. by D. W. Roberston, Jr. (New York.: Liberal Arts Press, 1958) p. 41.

[13] Francis Turretin, *Institutes of Elenctic Theology,* Vol. 1, trans. by George Musgrave Giger, ed. by James T. Dennison, Jr. (Phillipsburg: P & R, 1992) p. 156.

2

Sola Scriptura and the Early Church

James White

> In regard to the divine and holy mysteries of the faith, not the least part may be handed on without the Holy Scriptures. Do not be led astray by winning words and clever arguments. Even to me, who tell you these things, do not give ready belief, unless you receive from the Holy Scriptures the proof of the things which I announce. The salvation in which we believe is not proved from clever reasoning, but from the Holy Scriptures.[1]

If one did not know the source of these words, one could easily hear them being spoken by any Christian minister as he instructed a class of new believers. And yet these words were written over sixteen hundred years ago by Cyril of Jerusalem. Was his view unusual? Are modern Roman Catholic apologists correct when they call the doctrine of *sola scriptura* a "novelty"?

27

Or do we find many witnesses to a belief in the sufficiency of Scripture in the writings of these early leaders of the faith?

Remember the Real Issue

Before looking to the writings of the early church, it is important to remember the central issues that separate Protestants from Roman Catholics on the issue of the sufficiency of Scripture. While there are some modern Roman Catholic theologians who no longer profess as strident a position as that defined in official Roman documents, we cannot define Roman theology on the basis of a minority of modern theologians any more than Protestant theology can be defined by reference to a minority of liberal theologians.[2] The official documents of the Roman Catholic Church must define the issue at hand. The plainest statement on the part of Rome is found in the Council of Trent:

> It also clearly perceives that these truths and rules are contained in the written books and in the unwritten traditions, which, received by the Apostles themselves, the Holy Ghost dictating, have come down to us, transmitted as it were from hand to hand. Following, then, the examples of the orthodox Fathers, it re-

ceives and venerates with a feeling of piety and reverence all the books both of the Old and New Testaments, since one God is author of both; also the traditions, whether they relate to faith or to morals, as having been dictated either orally by Christ or by the Holy Ghost, and preserved in the Catholic Church in unbroken succession.[3]

The Roman claim is that "Sacred Tradition" exists in the "written books" *and* "in the unwritten traditions." These unwritten traditions, Rome claims, were received by the Apostles and preserved in the Roman Catholic Church in "unbroken succession." We are also told that the "orthodox Fathers" received and venerated *both* the written books *and* the unwritten traditions. Therefore, Rome has made the claim, as part of an infallible declaration of Roman dogma in the words of the Council of Trent, that the "orthodox Fathers" received and venerated *their idea* of tradition, *their idea* of "unwritten traditions"— revelation that is plainly divine in origin ("dictated . . . by Christ or by the Holy Ghost") and therefore necessary for anyone to have the full counsel of God. This fullness, we can readily see, can only be found in the bosom of Rome, the caretaker of this "other" part of God's revelation. When placed side by side, the two forms of tradition, written and oral, form one single

"Sacred Tradition"[4] according to Rome.

It is no surprise that modern defenders of Roman Catholicism have tried to avoid defending the strident claims of Trent. Just as modern Roman historians struggle to defend the pronunciations of Vatican I regarding papal infallibility, so the defenders of Trent are hard pressed to provide meaningful substantiation of that synod's extravagant claims. Specifically, demonstrating the existence of this inspired "oral tradition" that exists *outside of Scripture* and has been passed down from Christ and the apostles is a tall order. In fact, it is simply impossible, as no such thing exists. This is why some wish to view this "tradition" as merely interpretational in content, and deny it an inspired status.[5]

What has been the result of Rome's doctrine of tradition? One need only look at such concepts as papal infallibility and the Marian doctrines (Immaculate Conception and Bodily Assumption) to see how Rome has been willing to define *de fide* doctrine on the basis of this alleged "tradition." And with reference to Rome's view of the Bible, we take as an example the words of a popular writer, John O'Brien:

> Great as is our reverence for the Bible, reason and experience compel us to say that it alone is not a competent nor a safe guide as

to what we are to believe.[6]

A similar statement is found in the popular book *Where We Got the Bible* by Henry Graham:

> Venerable and inspired as Catholics regard the Bible, great as is their devotion to it for spiritual reading and support of doctrine, we yet do not pretend to lean upon it alone, as the Rule of faith and morals. Along with it we take that great Word that was never written, Tradition, and hold by both the one and the other interpreted by the living voice of the Catholic Church speaking through her Supreme Head, the infallible Vicar of Christ.[7]

The reader is encouraged to compare and contrast such a statement with the citations that will be provided from the early Fathers of the faith.

Proof-texting the Fathers

The person who wishes to know if the early Fathers provide *real* support for the *Roman* concept of "tradition" as defined above will recognize that a very specific kind of usage of the term is needed. Simply citing passages where the term "tradition" is found will hardly suffice, though this is, quite often, all that is offered to us.[8] Aside from the obvious consideration that the term "tradition" can carry many meanings,[9] it is plainly necessary to demonstrate that when an early Father refers to "tradition" he means by this the same concept as enunciated by Trent: an inspired tradition, passed down *outside of Scripture*, without which we do not and *cannot* have all of God's revealed truth.

I shall provide only two examples of how the early Fathers are often mistreated by Roman apologists in their quest to find support for their view of oral tradition. The first I draw from Irenaeus, bishop of Lyon (c. 130–c. 200). A number of his statements are often used to substantiate the existence of an extrabiblical "tradition" that we are told lends support to Roman claims. From his work, *Against Heresies*, we read:

> On this account are we bound to avoid *them,* but to make choice of the things pertaining to the Church with the utmost diligence, and to lay hold of the tradition of the truth. . . . For how should it be if the apostles themselves had not left us writings? Would it not be necessary [in that case] to follow the course of the tradition which they handed down to those to whom they did commit the Churches?[10]

Surely such a passage seems to speak of "tradition" as an extrabiblical thing, just as Trent. And this is not the only place where Irenaeus spoke thus. In the first part of the same work he had written:

> As I have already observed, the Church, having received this preaching and this faith, although scattered throughout the whole world, yet, as if occupying but one house, carefully preserves it. . . . For, although the languages of the world are dissimilar, yet the import of the tradition is one and the same.[11]

Citations such as these seem to carry great weight, until, that is, one looks more closely at the contexts. In both instances one discovers a very important fact. Our author did not fail to define for us exactly what this "tradition" was:

> These have all declared to us that there is one God, Creator of heaven and earth, announced by the law and the prophets; and one Christ, the Son of God. If any one does not agree to these truths, he despises the companions of the Lord; nay more, he despises Christ Himself the Lord; yea, he despises the Father also, and stands self-condemned, resisting and opposing his own salvation, as is the case with all heretics.[12]

Here is Irenaeus's "tradition," and we note immediately how it doesn't look anything like Rome's version. The important thing to see, aside from the fact that such items as papal infallibility and the Bodily Assumption of Mary are missing from Irenaeus' definition (items that Rome has defined on the basis of tradition), is that these truths *are derived from the Scriptures themselves*. There is not a single item listed by Irenaeus that cannot be demonstrated directly from the pages of Holy Writ. Hence, obviously, his idea of "tradition" provides Trent with no support at all, for Trent's definition does not assert a subscriptural, derivative summary of gospel truth, but an inspired revelation passed down orally through the episcopate. Irenaeus' view is not a Roman Catholic one.

Lest someone think that this is the only place where Irenaeus defined his tradition, we briefly note these words which follow *immediately* upon the heels of the first citation provided above:

> To which course many nations of those barbarians who believe in Christ do assent, having salvation written in their hearts by the Spirit, without paper or ink, and, carefully preserving the ancient tradition, believing in one God, the Creator of heaven and earth, and all things therein, by means of Christ Jesus, the Son of God; . . .[13]

Turning, then, from Irenaeus, we look to our second example, drawn from Basil of Caesarea (c. 330–379), the great Cappadocian Father. In his treatise *On the Spirit* Basil made the following famous remarks:

> Of the beliefs and practices whether generally accepted or publicly enjoined which are preserved in the Church some we possess derived from written teaching; others we have received delivered to us "in a mystery," by the tradition of the apostles; and both of these in relation to true religion have the same force. And these no one will gainsay;—no one, at all events, who is even moderately versed in the institutions of the Church. For were we to attempt to reject such customs as have no written authority, on the ground that the importance they possess is small, we should unintentionally injure the Gospel in its very vitals; or, rather, should make our public definition a mere phrase and nothing more.[14]

Surely here we have the Roman position, do we not? An extrabiblical "tradition" is here posited that would fit quite nicely with Trent, would it not? The importance of looking at all the data is again seen, for both the context and the greater scope of Basil's teaching contradict such a conclusion. First, we note the continua-

tion of his words, which are often not included
in the citation:

> For instance, to take the first and most
> general example, who is there who has
> taught us in writing to sign with the sign
> of the cross those who have trusted in the
> name of our Lord Jesus Christ? What
> writing has taught us to turn to the East at
> the prayer? Which of the saints has left us
> in writing the words of the invocation at
> the displaying of the bread of the Eucharist
> and the cup of blessing? For we are not, as
> is well known, content with what the apos-
> tle or the Gospel has recorded, but both in
> preface and conclusion we add other words
> as being of great importance to the validity
> of the ministry, and these we derive from
> unwritten teaching. Moreover we bless the
> water of baptism and the oil of the chrism,
> and besides this the catechuman who is
> being baptized. On what written authority
> do we do this? Is not our authority silent
> and mystical tradition? Nay, by what writ-
> ten word is the anointing of oil itself
> taught? And whence comes the custom of
> baptizing thrice?[15]

No matter how we might view Basil's beliefs,
one thing is certain: the matters that he lists as
being addressed by "tradition" are not the very
matters that Rome would have us to believe

comprise their "oral tradition." Basil is talking about traditions with reference to practices and piety. We note with some irony that Rome does not believe Basil is correct in his claims in this passage. Does Rome say we must face to the East at prayer? Does Rome insist upon triune baptism after the Eastern mode? Yet these are the *practices* that Basil defines as being derived from "tradition." What is more, other statements from this same Father fly in the face of the Roman claims. For example, when addressing truly important doctrinal truths, such as the very nature of God, Basil did not appeal to some nebulous tradition. How could he, especially when he encountered others who claimed that their traditional beliefs should be held as sacred? Note his words to Eustathius the physician:

> Their complaint is that their custom does not accept this, and that Scripture does not agree. What is my reply? I do not consider it fair that the custom which obtains among them should be regarded as a law and rule of orthodoxy. If custom is to be taken in proof of what is right, then it is certainly competent for me to put forward on my side the custom which obtains here. If they reject this, we are clearly not bound to follow them. Therefore let God-inspired

> Scripture decide between us; and on
> whichever side be found doctrines in har-
> mony with the word of God, in favor of that
> side will be cast the vote of truth.[16]

A sentiment hardly in line with Trent! This same Father also insisted, "The hearers taught in the Scriptures ought to test what is said by teachers and accept that which agrees with the Scriptures but reject that which is foreign. And in another place, "Plainly it is a falling away from faith and an offense chargeable to pride, either to reject any of those things that are written or to introduce things that are not written."[17] Just as plainly, then, Basil is not a friend of the Roman claims.[18]

Before moving on to other witnesses to the early belief in the sufficiency of Scripture without an additional "oral tradition" as defined by Rome, we need to note the problem posed by the patristic testimony. Protestants can greatly respect and learn from the early Fathers without investing them with infallibility. We can take the good while recognizing that they had their problems and failures, too. Hence, when we do find an early Father wandering from the path, we are not troubled or bothered by this. But for the Roman Catholic the situation is different. Rome's claims are fundamentally different, and hence a problem is raised by the presence, from the earliest periods of the church, of beliefs in the Fathers that are incompatible with what Rome alleges are in fact "apostolic" traditions and doctrines. And when the Protestant can go "toe to toe" with the Roman Catholic in citing the early Fathers, plainly the Roman position suffers, for she has to defend the idea that her traditions were "there" from the beginning, that hers is the "constant faith" of the Church.[19]

Patristic Testimonies

Space does not permit but a smattering of the testimony available to the person who wishes to allow the early Fathers to speak for themselves. We will content ourselves to hear first some of the words of the great bishop of Hippo, Augustine, and then we shall close by looking closely at the great defender of the Nicene faith, the bishop of Alexandria, Athanasius. We begin with samples of Augustine's view of the subject:

> What more shall I teach you than what we read in the apostle? For holy Scripture fixes the rule for our doctrine, lest we dare to be wiser than we ought. . . . Therefore, I should not teach you anything else except to expound to you the words of the Teacher.[20]

I must not press the authority of Nicea
against you, nor you that of Ariminum
against me; I do not acknowledge the one,
as you do not the other; but let us come to
ground that is common to both—the testimony of the Holy Scriptures.[21]

Let us not hear: This I say, this you say;
but, thus says the Lord. Surely it is the
books of the Lord on whose authority we
both agree and which we both believe.
There let us seek the church, there let us
discuss our case.[22]

Let those things be removed from our
midst which we quote against each other
not from divine canonical books but from
elsewhere. Someone may perhaps ask:
Why do you want to remove these things
from the midst? Because I do not want the
holy church proved by human documents
but by divine oracles.[23]

Whatever they may adduce, and wherever
they may quote from, let us rather, if we
are His sheep, hear the voice of our
Shepherd. Therefore let us search for the
church in the sacred canonical Scriptures.[24]

Neither dare one agree with catholic bishops if by chance they err in anything, with
the result that their opinion is against the

canonical Scriptures of God.[25]

> If anyone preaches either concerning
> Christ or concerning His church or con-
> cerning any other matter which pertains to
> our faith and life; I will not say, if we, but
> what Paul adds, if an angel from heaven
> should preach to you anything besides
> what you have received in the Scriptures
> of the Law and of the Gospels, let him be
> anathema.[26]

> You ought to notice particularly and store
> in your memory that God wanted to lay a
> firm foundation in the Scriptures against
> treacherous errors, a foundation against
> which no one dares to speak who would in
> any way be considered a Christian. For
> when He offered Him-self to them to touch,
> this did not suffice Him unless He also con-
> firmed the heart of the believers from the
> Scriptures, for He foresaw that the time
> would come when we would not have any-
> thing to touch but would have something
> to read.[27]

Are we to believe that Augustine *meant* to say,
in the immediately preceding quotation, "He
foresaw that the time would come when we
would not have anything to touch but would
have one thing to read, and another thing orally
passed on"? Did not Augustine make reference

to tradition? Yes, he did, but he did so in the
same context as Basil did above.[28]

Conflict is often a great and rich source of information regarding the beliefs of the early
Fathers. When faced with opposition the Fathers
"show their true colors," so to speak. How do
they handle the claims of their gainsayers? Do
they do as modern Roman Catholics and refer to
"tradition" as the basis of their doctrinal beliefs?
Or do we find them presenting the Scriptures as
their final and full authority?

No early Father answers this question more
clearly and with more power than Athanasius.
For years he stood against the combined might
of the Empire and the Church, firmly clinging to
the Nicene faith in the full deity of Jesus Christ.
For a time he even stood against the Roman See
under Liberius, the bishop of Rome who gave in
to the pressures placed upon him.[29] Truly it was
said of him, *Athanasius contra mundum*, "Athanasius against the world." What an amazingly
Protestant attitude was displayed by this bishop
of Alexandria! Against the weight of the combined Church he clung to the testimony of
Scripture, refuting his enemies not by reference
to some mythical oral "tradition," but by logical,
insightful exegesis of God-inspired Scripture.

We will begin by taking the opposition's

strongest objections and demonstrating that even here Athanasius fails them. Then we will provide just some of the numerous testimonies this rich source provides to our defense of *sola scriptura*. We begin by examining a passage that has been cited as evidence that Athanasius denied *sola scriptura*:

> But what is also to the point, let us note that the very tradition, teaching, and faith of the Catholic Church from the beginning, which the Lord gave, was preached by the Apostles, and was preserved by the Fathers. On this was the Church founded; and if anyone departs from this, he neither is nor any longer ought to be called a Christian.[30]

This section is quoted because it is surely liable to be read with modern eyes and understandings, is it not? "Aha!" comes the cry, "See! Athanasius speaks of tradition!" But, what does Athanasius *mean* by "tradition"? I will simply allow the quotation to continue so that he may speak for himself. What is this "tradition" that he is referring to?

> There is a Trinity, holy and perfect, acknowledged as God, in Father, Son, and Holy Spirit, having nothing foreign or ex-

ternal mixed with it, not composed of a
fashioner and an originated, but entirely
creative and fashioning. . . and thus there
is preached in the Church one God, "who is
over all, and through all, and in all. . . ."
And because this is the faith of the Church,
let them somehow understand that the
Lord sent out the Apostles and commanded
them to make this the foundation of the
Church, when He said: "Go out and instruct every people, baptizing them in the
name of the Father and of the Son and of
the Holy Spirit."[31]

This is very important, for it is beyond dispute that Athanasius develops, *and defends*, the
Trinity on the basis of Scripture. He does not
appeal for this truth to some unwritten revelation that exists *outside* of Scripture, that contains
revelation not found in Scripture. This must be
taken into consideration when defining his view
of the term "tradition" and what it includes.
This "tradition," we see then, is secondary to
and subordinate to the Scriptures.[32]

Another passage that is often urged against
the many plain testimonies we will present from
Athanasius is as follows:

That of what they now allege from the
Gospels they certainly give unsound interpretation, we may easily see, if we now

> consider the scope of that faith which we
> Christians hold, and using it as a rule, ap-
> ply ourselves, as the Apostle teaches, to
> the reading of the inspired Scripture. For
> Christ's enemies, being ignorant of this
> scope, have wandered from the way of
> truth. . . .[33]

Roman apologists point to the term "scope"[34] and say, "Here is a rule that Athanasius refers to that violates any concept of *sola scriptura.*" And again, taken alone, one can see how such a conclusion could be drawn. But this passage does not exist alone. It is in the third discourse of four written by Athanasius against the Arians. Prior to getting to this point Athanasius has addressed a wide range of topics. Indeed, in the first discourse he came to a point that would have provided him the perfect opportunity of singing the praises of "oral tradition." He wrote,

> If such bewilderment and empty speaking
> be from ignorance, Scripture will teach
> them, that the devil, the author of heresies,
> because of the ill savour which attaches to
> evil, borrows Scripture language, as a cloak
> wherewith to sow the ground with his own
> poison also, and to seduce the simple.[35]

How do modern Roman apologists handle statements made by heretics claiming Scriptural

backing? Do they not quickly refer to the need of
something *more* than Scripture? Do we not often
see the cults and "isms" used as examples of
why *sola scriptura* doesn't work? Yet we don't
find any such song of praise to "oral tradition"
here in Athanasius. Instead, we find Athanasius
saying, "For, behold, we take divine Scripture
and thence discourse with freedom of the religious Faith. . . ."[36] And at the beginning of the
next paragraph:

> Which of the two theologies sets forth our
> Lord Jesus Christ as God and Son of the
> Father, this which you vomited forth, or
> that which we have spoken and maintain
> from the Scriptures?

Which is followed closely by the following:

> For if they speak, a condemnation will fol-
> low; and if they be suspected, proofs from
> Scripture will be cast at them from every
> side.

Scripture proofs? Why not just throw the
weight of oral tradition at them and be done
with it? That is surely how one must handle
such doctrines as papal infallibility and the
Bodily Assumption! But this is not Athanasius's
way. Instead, he shows the consistency of his

own belief with Scripture, and the inconsistency of the heretics' beliefs, all in accord with the same standard:

> Nor does Scripture afford them any pretext; for it has been often shown, and it shall be shown now, that their doctrine is alien to the divine oracles.[37]

What follows this is yet another lengthy discussion of the Son's eternity, all taken, without exception, from Scripture itself, so that he concludes,

> It is plain then from the above that the Scriptures declare the Son's eternity.[38]

The rest of the first discourse is taken up with providing an orthodox interpretation of various passages put forth by the heretics. Here again we have an opportunity of seeing Athanasius's view of authority, for this section begins thus:

> But since they allege the divine oracles and force on them a misinterpretation, according to their private sense, it becomes necessary to meet them just so far as to vindicate these passages, and to show that they bear an orthodox sense, and that our opponents are in error.[39]

And how does Athanasius do this? Does he
appeal to unwritten tradition to prove that the
interpretation of the heretics is in error? No. He
exegetes the passages themselves, and shows
the inconsistencies of the Arian interpretations.
Just as I would reply to a Jehovah's Witness
who would use the same passages, Athanasius
did 1500 years ago.

We press on to the above-cited section of this
discourse. As we have already seen, context is a
vital aspect of citing the Fathers. In this in-
stance, the meaning of the term "scope" is defined further in the very next paragraph:

> Now the scope and character of Holy
> Scripture, as we have often said, is this—it
> contains a double account of the Saviour;
> that He was ever God, and is the Son, be-
> ing the Father's Word and Radiance and
> Wisdom; and that afterwards for us He took
> flesh of a Virgin, Mary Bearer of God, and
> was made man. And this scope is to be
> found throughout inspired Scripture, as
> the Lord Himself has said, "Search the
> Scriptures, for they are they which testify
> of Me."[40]

This "scope," we are told, "is to be found
throughout inspired Scripture." Obviously, therefore, it is not something that exists *separately*

from Scripture. Just as I might say, "The concept of the sovereignty of God is a belief that is to be found throughout Scripture," Athanasius refers to the truth of the nature of Christ in the same way. Therefore, this "scope" does not qualify for the Roman concept of oral tradition, and Athanasius is not found to be violating the doctrine of *sola scriptura*.

What then of the positive testimony from Athanasius? We note first and foremost the plain words from his work against the heathen:

> For indeed the holy and God-breathed Scriptures are self-sufficient for the preaching of the truth.[41]

In this passage Athanasius begins with a fundamental tenet of his faith: the full sufficiency of Scripture for the proclamation of the truth. He immediately goes on to note that God uses other sources to teach truth as well, including godly men with an insight into Scripture. But he begins where Protestants and Roman Catholics part company: with the sufficiency of Scripture. He had learned such things from those who came before him. He even mentions the words of Antony, "The Scriptures are enough for instruction, but it is a good thing to encourage one another in the faith, and to stir up with words."[42] When writing to the Egyptian bishops he asserted:

> But since holy Scripture is of all things most sufficient for us, therefore recommending to those who desire to know more of these matters, to read the Divine word, I now hasten to set before you that which most claims attention, and for the sake of which principally I have written these things.[43]

The high view of Scripture is continued in this passage from Athanasius's work on the Incarnation of the Word of God:

> Let this, then, Christ-loving man, be our offering to you, just for a rudimentary sketch and outline, in a short compass, of the faith of Christ and of His Divine appearing usward. But you, taking occasion by this, if you light upon the text of the Scriptures, by genuinely applying your mind to them, will learn from them more completely and clearly the exact detail of what we have said. For they were spoken and written by God, through men who spoke for God.[44]

One will search in vain for a reference wherein this Father describes "oral tradition" in such a way, and yet Trent did not fear to so speak of "tradition." Rather than finding O'Brien's idea that Scripture is not a "safe guide" as to what we are to believe, Athanasius said: ". . . for the tokens of truth are more exact as drawn from Scripture, than from other sources."[45] These "other sources" included church councils, such as that of Nicea, which Athanasius defended so strongly. Yet he realized that his sufficiency was not based upon the alleged authority of a council, but that the power of that council came from its fidelity to Scripture. Note his words with reference to the Arians:

> Vainly then do they run about with the pretext that they have demanded Councils for the faith's sake; for divine Scripture is sufficient above all things; but if a Council be needed on the point, there are the proceedings of the Fathers, for the Nicene Bishops did not neglect this matter, but stated the doctrines so exactly, that persons reading their words honestly, cannot but be reminded by them of the religion towards Christ announced in divine Scripture.[46]

By now the phrase "for divine Scripture is sufficient above all things" should be familiar, as it is a constant thread in Athanasius' writings. And it is vital to note that the weight of the Nicene Council is described in terms of the *consistency* of the Council's teachings with the "religion towards Christ announced in divine Scripture."

Conclusions

What can we conclude from our brief review of just some of the available patristic material? We first note that the traditional Roman Catholic position regarding a separate "oral tradition" is not the unanimous, nor the ancient, nor the constant faith of the Church. The idea that the Scriptures are insufficient, lacking an important counterbalance in the oral tradition, and are incompetent to function as a guide as to what we are to believe, is obviously the "theological novum," the later development, the departure from the ancient faith. Yet we find Roman Catholic apologists trying to make it sound as if *sola scriptura* is the innovation.

In the process of attacking *sola scriptura*, Roman apologists are forced to badly misrepresent the patristic materials, and engage in what I call "anachronistic interpretation," the reading back into ancient sources concepts and ideas that were not a part of the original context at all. Rome does this with almost every one of her unique—and false—doctrines (the Papacy, the Marian doctrines, etc.). Sadly, however, many Protestants are taken in by these arguments. Most Protestants are ahistorical in their view of the church, and have little, if any, knowledge of church history. Even those with some training often fail to take the time to examine the original sources from which Roman apologists derive their out-of-context citations. If we take the time to clearly recognize exactly what Rome is claiming, and then look to the patristic sources, we find a glaring inconsistency. Rome's claims to historical foundation are missing, not only here with reference to *sola scriptura*, but for all her unique, later-developing dogmas that she lays upon men under pain of the anathema.

As with all elements of Christian truth, full examination will always support, uphold, and verify. *Sola scriptura* has long been the rule of believing Christian people, even before it became necessary to use the specific terminology against later innovators who would usurp the Scriptures' supremacy in the church. It is the teaching of the Scriptures about themselves (2 Timothy 3:16–17, Matthew 15:1–9, etc.), and we find a broad and deep witness to it in the early Fathers of the faith, as we have seen. Let us be thankful to God for the gracious gift of His sufficient and life-giving Word, the Holy Scriptures.

---

1 Cyril of Jerusalem, *Catechetical Lectures* 4:17. An alternate translation can be found in Schaff and Wace, *A Select Library of Nicene and Post-Nicene Fathers of the Christian Church* (hereafter *NPNF*), Series II (Grand Rapids.: Eerdmans, 1980) VII:23.

2 The reader is encouraged to see Robert Strimple's essay, "The Relationship Between Scripture and Tradition in Contemporary Roman Catholic Theology" (*Westminster Theological Journal*, Fall 1977, 40:22–38), for an excellent summary of the positions of many of these modern Roman Catholics who deny the more traditional Roman view of *partim-partim*, that is, "partly-partly," partly in Scripture, partly in tradition. Strimple points out that many of the Roman Catholic theologians who are referred to as being "progressive" in the sense of denying the *partim-partim* concept are, in point of fact, *farther* away from a conservative Protestant position due to their post-Enlightenment view of revelation as a whole.

3 Translation by Rev. H. J. Schroeder in *The Canons and Decrees of the Council of Trent* (Rockford, Ill.: TAN Books, 1978), p. 17. For the Latin of the text see Philip Schaff, *The Creeds of Christendom* (Grand Rapids.: Baker, 1985), II:80.

4 Roman Catholic writings are filled with ambiguities regarding the exact nature of "tradition." Even the difference of capitalization can be significant. For example, while many Roman writers use "Sacred Tradition" to represent both the oral and written combined, Vatican II used the uncapitalized form, "sacred tradition," to refer to the oral in distinction from the written: "Consequently, it is not from sacred Scripture alone that the Church draws her certainty about everything which has been revealed. Therefore both sacred tra-

dition and sacred Scripture are to be accepted and venerated with the same sense of devotion and reverence" (*Dei Verbum* 9). And, "Sacred tradition and sacred Scripture form one sacred deposit or the word of God, which is committed to the Church. . . . She has always regarded the Scriptures together with sacred tradition as the supreme rule of faith, and will ever do so" (*Dei Verbum* 10, 21).

5 Just how empty the claim of "material sufficiency" on the part of Roman apologists really is can be readily seen in these words from John Hardon, *The Catholic Catechism* (New York: Doubleday, 1975), p. 161, in which he describes the source of the dogma of the Assumption of Mary:

> Pope Pius defined Mary's Assumption as a truth divinely revealed. Of the two sources of revelation, theologians commonly say the Assumption was implicit in Tradition, in spite of the practical absence of documentary evidence before A.D. 300. Yet the Pope finally declared that the doctrine was in revelation. How do we know? On the answer to this question rests a new insight into Christian Tradition that has been gaining momentum since the eighteenth century. Briefly stated, Tradition is coming to be identified more with the Church's magisterium or teaching office and less exclusively as the source along with Scripture of the truths of salvation. . . . "Together with the sources of revelation (Scripture and Tradition) God has given to his Church a living magisterium to elucidate and explain what is contained in the deposit of faith only obscurely, and, as it were, by implication." The degree of obscurity, we may add, is unimportant. Given this

faculty by her founder, whose Spirit of truth abides
with her at all times, the Church can infallibly discern what belongs to revelation no matter how cryptic
the contents may be.

What is gained by taking such a view? The Roman apologist does
not have to defend the idea of an inspired oral tradition, but he now
has to defend the idea that the Roman magisterium herself is so divinely guided that she can "infallibly discern" what is, and what is
not, revelation, and that no matter what the "degree of obscurity"
with which such a divine truth may be cloaked! On the practical
level, what this means is really worse than the traditional view:
Rome can "find" whatever she wishes to find in "revelation," and
impose this alleged "truth" upon all believers, and that with the
pain of the anathema. She did just that with the Assumption of
Mary, a doctrine utterly absent from Scripture *and* early church history. Yet, it is a belief that must be embraced *de fide,* and, in the
words of Pope Pius IX, "if some should think in their hearts otherwise than we have defined (which God forbid), they shall know and
thoroughly understand that they are by their own judgment condemned, have made shipwreck concerning the faith, and fallen away
from the unity of the Church; and, moreover, that they, by this very
act, subject themselves to the penalties ordained by law, if, by word
or writing, or any other external means, they dare to signify what
they think in their hearts." Roman apologists who take this view are
not arguing for "Scripture and tradition." They are, in reality,
arguing for "Scripture and Church."

6 John O'Brien, *Finding Christ's Church* (Notre Dame, Ind.: Ave Maria
Press, 1950), p. 18.

7 Henry G. Graham, *Where We Got the Bible* (Rockford, Ill: TAN

Books, 1977), p. 152.

8 For example, see the section "The Fathers Know Best" in *This Rock*, the magazine of the Roman Catholic apologetics organization *Catholic Answers*, October 1990, pp. 21–22.

9 Martin Chemnitz identified and illustrated at least eight different uses of the term "tradition" in patristic sources in his *Examination of the Council of Trent* (St. Louis: Concordia Publishing House, 1971), I:219–307.

10 Irenaeus, *Against Heresies*, 3, 4:1. See Alexander Roberts and James Donaldson, editors, *The Ante-Nicene Fathers* (Grand Rapids: Eerdmans, 1981), I:416–417. This passage is cited in the article, "Traditions of God, Not Men" from *This Rock*.

11 Ibid., 1, 10:2.

12 Ibid., 3, 1:1. It is important to point out why Irenaeus was so concerned about the "tradition" teaching that there is one God who created all things by Jesus Christ. He was struggling against Gnosticism, a system that denied that the one true God created all things. Instead, the Gnostics posited intermediate beings between the one true God and the creation.

13 Ibid., 3, 4:2. The same is true of the citation from *Against Heresies*, 1, 10:2—this tradition is clearly laid out in full in 1, 10:1, and that replete with numerous direct citations of Scripture!

14 Basil, *On the Spirit*, 66 in *NPNF*, Series II, VIII:40–41. This same passage is cited in the *This Rock* article, beginning and ending at the same point.

15 Ibid.

16 *NPNF*, Series II, VIII:229. See also Basil's defense of the Trinity and his reliance fully upon "God-inspired Scripture," not "oral tradition," in such places as his letter to Gregory found in the same volume, pp. 137–141, particularly section 4.

17 As given by the Roman Catholic source, William Jurgens, *The Faith of the Early Fathers* (Collegeville, Minn.: Liturgical Press, 1979), II:24. Jurgens provides a most enlightening note to this passage: "The terms ἀθετεῖν τι τῶν γεγραμμένων and ἐπεισάγειν τῶν μνὴ γεγραμμένων may be taken as equivalent to 'to reject anything that is in Scripture' and 'to introduce anything that is not in Scripture.' "

18 One might note in passing the fact that both Fathers thus far reviewed are also problems for Roman claims regarding papal supremacy, Irenaeus in his rebuke of Victor, and Basil in his rejection of Rome's interference in the matter of Meletius of Antioch. For the text of Irenaeus's rebuke of Victor, see *The Ante-Nicene Fathers*, I:569, and for Basil's siding with Meletius against Rome, see *NPNF*, Series II, VIII:253.

19 Phrases like "the constant faith of the Church" and the "unanimous consent of the Fathers" are drawn directly from the claims of Trent and Vatican I.

20 Augustine, *De bono viduitatis*, 2. See *NPNF*, Series I, III:442 for alternate translation. Migne (*PL* 40:431) provides the text: "Quam id quod apud Apostolum legimus? Sancta enim Scriptura nostræ docrtinæ regulum figit, ne audeamus *sapere plus quam oportet sapere;*. . . . Non sit ergo mihi aliud te docere, nisi verba tibi doctoris exponere." Note especially the use of the phrase, "Scriptura nostræ doctrinæ regulam figit," for *sola scriptura* is the doctrine that teaches that Scripture is the sole infallible and supreme "regula fidei," the "rule of faith," for the Church.

21 Augustine, "To Maximin the Arian," as cited by George Salmon,

---

The Infallibility of the Church (Grand Rapids.: Baker, 1959), p. 295. Salmon gives the text as, "Sed nun nec ego Nicaenum, nec tu debes Ariminense, tanquam praejudicaturus, proferre concilium. Nec ego hujus auctoritate, ne tu illius detineris. Scripturarum auctoritatibus, non quorumque propriis, sed utrique communibus testibus, res cum re, causa cum causa, ratio cum ratione concertet" (Augustine, *Cont. Maximin. Arian.* ii. 14, vol. VIII:704).

22 Augustine, *De unitate ecclesiae*, 3, as cited by Martin Chemnitz, *Examination of the Council of Trent,* Part I (St. Louis: Concordia Publishing House, 1971), p. 157.

23 Ibid.

24 Ibid.

25 Ibid., 10, cited by Chemnitz, p. 159.

26 Augustine, *Contra litteras Petiliani*, Bk 3, ch. 6. Migne (PL 43:351) provides the text: "Proinde sive de Christo, sive de ejus Ecclesia, sive de quacumque alia re quæ pertinet ad fidem vitamque vestram, non dicam nos, nequaquam comparandi ei qui dixit, *Licet si nos*; sed omnino quod secutus adjecit, *Si angelus de cælo vobis annuntiaverit præter quam quod* in Scripturis legalibus et evangelicis *accepistis, anathema sit.*"

27 Augustine, *In Epistolam Johannis tractus*, 2. See *NPNF* Series I, VII:469. The final phrase in Latin is, "in quo quod palpemus nos non habemus, sed quod legamus habemus" (Migne, PL 35:1989).

28 See especially Augustine's letter to Januarius for a full discussion of his view on this point (*NPNF*, Series I, I:300–303). Note especially the fact that Augustine himself differentiates between those practices based upon Scripture and those based upon "tradition" (Chapter 6).

29 See the discussion of Liberius and the entire concept of papal infallibility in Philip Schaff, *The Creeds of Christendom* (Grand Rapids.: Baker, 1985), I:134–188, and his *History of the Christian Church* (Grand Rapids: Eerdmans, 1985), III:635–636, especially footnote 2.

30 Athanasius, *To Serapion*, 1, 28, as cited in Jurgens, *The Faith of the Early Fathers*, I:336. Text in Migne, *Patrologiæ Cursus Completus, Series Græca* (1857), 26:593–596 (hereafter, *PG*).

31 Ibid.

32 Compare the use of the phrase "subordinate standards" with reference to various Protestant confessions as an example of the modern use of this concept.

33 Athanasius, *Four Discourses Against the Arians*, III:28, in *NPNF*, Series II, IV:409. Text in Migne, *PG*, 26:384–385.

34 Greek is σκοπό.

35 *NPNF*, IV:310; Migne, *PG*, 26:25.

36 *NPNF*, IV:311; Migne, *PG*, 26:28.

37 *NPNF*, IV:312; Migne, *PG*, 26:33.

38 *NPNF*, IV:313; Migne, *PG*, 26:37.

39 *NPNF*, IV:327–328; Migne, *PG*, 26:88.

40 *NPNF*, IV:409; Migne, *PG*, 26:385.

41 Translation by the author. Greek text found in Robert Thomson, editor, *Athanasius: Contra Gentes and De Incarnatione* (Oxford:

Clarendon Press, 1971), p. 2. Or Migne, *PG*, 25:4. The Greek reads, αὐτάρκεις μὲν γάρ εἰσιν αἱ ἅγιαι καὶ θεόπνευστοι γραφαὶ πρὸς τὴν τῆς ἀληθείας ἀπαγγελίαν. With reference to the term αὐτάρκεις, we note the definition provided by Bauer, "sufficiency, a competence" and "contentment, self-sufficiency." See Bauer, Arndt, Gingrich, and Danker, *A Greek-English Lexicon of the New Testament and Other Early Christian Literature*, 2nd ed. (Chicago: University of Chicago Press, 1979), p. 122. The most helpful work of Louw and Nida, *Greek-English Lexicon of the New Testament Based on Semantic Domains* (United Bible Societies: 1988), p. 680, says of the term, "a state of adequacy or sufficiency—'what is adequate, what is sufficient, what is needed, adequacy. . . .' In a number of languages the equivalent of this expression in 2 Corinthians 9:8 may be 'always having all that you need' or, stated negatively, 'not lacking in anything.' "

42 Athanasius, *Vita S. Antoni*, 16, *NPNF*, Series II, IV:200. The Greek text reads, τὰς μὲν γραφὰς ἱκανὰς εἶναι πρὸς διδασκαλίαν (Cited by E. P. Meijering, *Athanasius: Contra Gentes* (Leiden: E. J. Brill, 1984), p. 10; Migne, *PG*, 26:868. One cannot help but notice the close parallel to Paul's words in 2 Timothy 3:16, where he writes that the God-breathed Scriptures are ὠφέλιμος προς διδασκαλίαν. Roman apologists try to weaken the term ὠφέλιμος as much as possible, asserting that Scripture is *merely* profitable. It is interesting to note how Athanasius obviously understands the meaning of ὠφέλιμος to be parallel with ἱκανὰς, a term that plainly speaks of sufficiency (see next note).

43 Athanasius, *Ad Episcopos Ægyptiæ*, in *NPNF*, Series II, IV:225. The Greek text is found in Migne, PG, 25:548. It reads, Ἐπειδὴ δὲ ἡ θεία Γραφὴ πάντων ἐστιν ἱκανωτέρα, τούτου χάριν τοῖς βουλεμένοις τὰ πολλὰ περὶ τούτων γινώσκειν συμβουλεύσας ἐντυγχάνειν τοῖς θείοις λόγοις, αὐτὸς νῦν τὸ κατεπεῖγον ἐσπούδασα δηλῶσαι, διὸ μάλιστα καὶ οὕτως ἔγραψα. The term Athanasius uses here to describe the sufficiency of Scripture is ἱκανωτέρα. The comparative form used here is translated as "of all things most sufficient," or "is more sufficient than all things." The substantival form is defined as

"fitness, capability, qualification" by Bauer; the adjectival form, "sufficient, adequate, large enough"; the verbal form, "make sufficient, qualify"; and the adverbial form, "sufficiently" (Bauer, *Greek-English Lexicon,* p. 374). So common is Athanasius's usage of both ἱκανα and αὐτάρκεις (see notes 41 and 42) with reference to Scripture that he combines them in his letter to Serapion (1:19; Migne, *PG*, 26:573) as follows: μόνον τὰ ἐν ταῖς Γραφαῖς μανθανέτω. Αὐτάρκη γὰρ καὶ ἱκανὰ τὰ ἐν ταύταις κείμενα ("Let us learn only the things that are in Scripture. For sufficient and adequate are the things therein"). Roman apologists must utterly reject Athanasius's obvious understanding of the term "profitable" in 2 Timothy 3:16 as referring to sufficiency and adequacy.

44 Athanasius, *De Incarnatione Verbi Dei,* 56, in *NPNF,* Series II, IV:66. The final phrase is, ἐκεῖναι μὲν γὰρ διὰ θεολόγων ἀνδρῶν παρὰ θεοῦ ἐλαλήθησαν καὶ ἐγράφησαν. Text in Meijering, *Athanasius: Contra Gentes,* p. 10, and Migne, *PG,* 25:196.

45 Athanasius, *De Decretis,* 32, in *NPNF,* Series II, IV:172; Migne, *PG,* 25:476.

46 Athanasius, *De Synodis,* 6, in *NPNF,* II, IV:453; Migne, *PG,* 26:689. The text regarding the sufficiency of Scripture is familiar by now: Ἔστι μὲν γὰρ ἱκανωτερ[α] πάντων ἡ θεία Γραφή.

3

The Establishment of Scripture

Dr. R. C. Sproul

"Norm of norms and without norm." With these words the historic church confessed her faith in the authority of Sacred Scripture. The phrase "norm of norms" was designed to indicate the superlative degree in a manner similar to that expression used in the New Testament for Christ, that He is King of kings and "Lord of lords." To be King of kings is to be the supreme King who rules over all lesser kings. To be Lord of lords is to be exalted above all other lords. Likewise the phrase "norm of norms" indicates a norm that is over lesser norms. The additional phrase, "without norm," indicates that the normative character of Scripture is a norm *sui generis*. This norm is in a class by itself. It does not function as a *primus inter pares*, a first among equals.

When we speak of the Canon of Scripture we are speaking of a norm or rule. The term

"canon" is derived by transliteration from the
Greek word *kanon*, which means "a measuring
rod," "rule," or "norm." In popular usage the
term Canon refers to the collection of individual
books that together comprise the Old and New
Testaments. It is the complete list of books that
is received by the Church and is codified into
what we call the Bible. The word "Bible" comes
from the Greek word for "book." Strictly speaking the Bible is not a book, but a collection of
sixty-six books. At least the classical Protestant
Bible contains sixty-six books. The Roman Catholic Bible includes the Apocrypha and is therefore larger than sixty-six books. This points to
the ongoing debate as to the precise nature of
the Canon. Rome and historic Protestantism dis-
agree about the proper makeup of the biblical
Canon. Protestant Creeds exclude the Apocrypha
from the Canon.

This disagreement about the Apocrypha
points to the larger issue that surrounds the
question of Canon. How was the Canon established? By whose authority? Is the Canon closed
to further additions? These and other questions
attend the broader issue of the nature of the biblical Canon.

One of the most important questions regarding the Canon is the question of its historical

compilation. Did the Canon come into being by the fiat of the church? Was it already in existence in the primitive Christian community? Was the Canon established by a special Providence? Is it possible that certain books that made their way into the present Canon should not have been included? Is it possible that books that were excluded should have been included?

We know that at least for a temporary period Luther raised questions about the inclusion of the Epistle of James in the New Testament Canon. That Luther once referred to James as an "Epistle of Straw" or a "Right strawy Epistle" is a matter of record. Critics of biblical inspiration have not grown weary of pointing to these comments of Luther to argue their case that Luther did not believe in the inspiration or infallibility of Scripture. This argument not only fails to do justice to Luther's repeated assertions of the divine authority of Scripture and their freedom from error, but more seriously it fails to make the proper distinction between the question of the nature of Scripture and the extent of Scripture. Luther was unambiguous in his conviction that all of Scripture is inspired and infallible. His question about James was not a question of the inspiration of Scripture but a question of whether James was in fact Scripture.

Though Luther did not challenge the infallibility of Scripture he most emphatically challenged the infallibility of the church. He allowed
for the possibility that the church could err, even
when the church ruled on the question of what
books properly belonged in the Canon. To see
this issue more clearly we can refer to a distinction often made by Dr. John Gerstner. Gerstner
distinguishes between the Roman Catholic view
of the Canon and the Protestant view of the
Canon in this manner:

ROMAN CATHOLIC VIEW: The Bible is an infallible collection of infallible books.

PROTESTANT VIEW: The Bible is a fallible collection of infallible books.

The distinction in view here refers to the
Catholic Church's conviction that the Canon of
Scripture was declared infallibly by the church.
On the other hand, the Protestant view is that
the church's decision regarding what books
make up the Canon was a fallible decision.
Being fallible means that it is possible that the
church erred in its compilation of the books
found in the present Canon of Scripture.
When Gerstner makes this distinction he is

neither asserting nor implying that the church indeed *did* err in its judgment of what properly belongs to the Canon. His view is not designed to cast doubt on the Canon but simply to guard against the idea of an infallible church. It is one thing to say that the church *could* have erred; it is another thing to say that the church *did* err.

Gerstner's formula has often been met with both consternation and sharp criticism in evangelical circles. It seems to indicate that he and those who agree with his assessment are undermining the authority of the Bible. But nothing could be further from the truth. Like Luther and Calvin before him, Gerstner has been an ardent defender of the infallibility and inerrancy of Scripture. His formula is merely designed to acknowledge that there was a historical selection process by which the church determined what books were really Scripture and what books were not Scripture. The point is that in this sifting or selection process the church sought to identify what books were actually to be regarded as Scripture.

It may be said that Rome has a certain "advantage" with respect to infallibility. Rome believes that the church is infallible as well as the Scripture. This infallibility extends not only to the question of Canon formation but also to the question of Biblical interpretation. To summarize, we can say that according to Rome we have an infallible Bible whose extent is decreed infallibly by the church and whose content is interpreted infallibly by the church. The Christian individual is still left in his own fallibility as he seeks to understand the infallible Bible as interpreted by the infallible church. No one is extending infallibility to the individual believer.

For the classic Protestant, though the individual believer has the right to the private interpretation of Scripture, it is clearly acknowledged that the individual is capable of misinterpreting the Bible. He has the ability to misinterpret Scripture, but never the right to do it. That is, with the right of private interpretation the responsibility of correct interpretation is also given. We never have the right to distort the teaching of Scripture. Both sides agree that the individual is fallible when seeking to understand the Scripture. Historic Protestantism limits the scope of infallibility to the Scriptures themselves. Church tradition and church creeds can err. Individual interpreters of Scripture can err. It is the Scriptures alone that are without error.

Though it is clear that the church went through a selection or sorting process in establishing a formal list of the Canonical books this does not mean that there was no Canon or rule prior to the decisions of church councils. The New Testament writings served as a functional Canon from the beginning. B. B. Warfield remarks:

> The church did not grow up by natural law: it was founded. And the authoritative teachers sent forth by Christ to found His church carried with them, as their most precious possession, a body of divine Scriptures, which they imposed on the church that they founded as its code of law. No reader of the New Testament can need proof of this; on every page of that book is spread the evidence that from the very beginning the Old Testament was as cordially recognized as law by the Christian as by the Jew. The Christian church thus was never without a "Bible" or a "canon."[1]

Warfield's point that the church was founded calls attention to the fact that the church had a founder and a foundation. The founder was Christ. The foundation was the writings of the prophets and the apostles. In the image of the church as a building the metaphor views Christ as the chief cornerstone. He is not the foundation of the church. He is the founder. The foundation of the church is laid by Christ and in Christ. He is the Chief Cornerstone in which this foundation is laid. Again it is the prophets and the Apostles who are called the foundation in the building metaphor.

The Canon of the New Testament rests upon a "tradition." The term "tradition" is often viewed by a jaundiced eye among Evangelicals. It suffers from the problem of guilt by association. In order to distance itself from the role played by tradition in Rome, zealous Evangelicals face the danger of throwing out the baby with the bath water. The Reformation principle of *Sola Scriptura* emphatically rejects the dual-source theory of Rome with respect to special revelation. At the Fourth Session of the Council of Trent, Rome declared that the truth of God is found both in the Scriptures and in the tradition of the church. The Reformers rejected this dual source and refused to elevate church tradition to such a high level.

Christ rebuked the Pharisees for supplanting the word of God with the traditions of men. This negative judgment of human tradition coupled with the aversion to the Roman Catholic view of tradition has inclined some Evangelicals to reject tradition altogether. The danger in this is to miss the important role tradition plays within the scope of Scripture itself. Scripture does not reject all tradition. It repudiates the traditions of men, but affirms another tradition—the divine tradition. Paul, for example, frequently speaks of tradition in a positive sense. He speaks of that body of truth that was given over to the church by Christ and the Apostles. This is the *paradosis*, the "giving over" of the truth of God.

The positive tradition of which Scripture speaks may be referred to as the Apostolic Tradition, which tradition played heavily on the formation of the Canon. The church did not create a new tradition by the establishing of the Canon. Indeed it is not really proper to speak of the establishing of the Canon by the church. It is not the church that established the Canon; it is the Canon that established the church. The church did not establish the Canon but recognized it and submitted to its rule.

At the heart of the Canon question is the issue of apostolic authority. In the New Testament the apostle (*apostolos*) is "one who is sent." The office of the apostle carries with it the delegated authority of the One who sends or authorizes the apostle to speak in His behalf. The apostolic tradition begins with God the Father. The Father is the One who first commissioned an apostle. The first apostle in the New Testament is Christ

Himself as He is sent by the Father and speaks
with the Father's delegated authority. It is to
Christ that the Father gives "all authority on
heaven and on earth." The second apostle is the
Holy Spirit who is sent by both the Father and
the Son. Next in line of delegated authority are
the New Testament apostles such as Peter and
Paul (and the rest).

In the patristic period of church history
Irenaeus understood this linkage. In defending
the apostles over against heretics, Irenaeus argued that to reject the apostles was to reject the
One who sent them, namely Christ. To reject
Christ is to reject the One who sent Him,
namely God the Father. Thus, for Irenaeus to reject the apostolic teaching was to reject God. At
this point Irenaeus was merely echoing the
words of Jesus when He said to His apostles
that whoever received them received Him and
whoever rejected them rejected Him.

It was the apostolic tradition that was codified in the formalization of the New Testament
Canon. The apostolic tradition was not limited
to the writings of the apostles themselves exclusively. Rather the Canon of Scripture contains
the writings of the apostles and their *companions*.
Again Warfield comments:

Let it, however, be clearly understood that it was not exactly apostolic *authorship* which, in the estimation of the earliest churches, constituted a book or portion of the "canon." Apostolic authorship was, indeed, early confounded with canonicity. It was doubt as to the apostolic authorship of Hebrews, in the West, and of James and Jude, apparently, which underlies the slowness of the inclusion of these books in the "canon" of certain churches. But from the beginning it was not so. The principle of canonicity was not apostolic authorship, but *imposition by the apostles as "law."* Hence Tertullian's name for the "canon" is *instrumentum*; and he speaks of the Old and New *Instrument* as we would of the Old and New Testament.[2]

That the church had a "functional canon" from the beginning is seen from the writings of the New Testament itself. Peter, in 68 A.D., refers to Paul's writings as being included among the "other Scriptures" (2 Peter 3:16). Paul also quotes from Luke's Gospel in 1 Timothy 5:18. From the earliest period of the post-apostolic age the church fathers treated the New Testament writings as Scripture. Though the early fathers did not customarily use the word "Scripture," they treated the apostolic writings with Scriptural authority. Quotations taken from the writings of the New Testament and cited as authorities may be found in the writings of Clement, Ignatius, Polycarp, Papias, Justin Martyr, and others.

Toward the end of the second century Tatian's *Diatessaron* contained a harmony of the Gospels. The Muratorian Canon (probably of the late second century) contained a list of New Testament books that perhaps was aimed to counter the false canon created by the heretic Marcion. Marcion's canon was a deliberate attempt to give an expurgated version of the New Testament to accommodate his negative view of the Old Testament God. Marcion's "New Testament" included the Gospel of Luke and ten of Paul's Epistles.

From the earliest period of her history it is clear that the vast majority of the books that are now contained in the New Testament Canon were functioning as "Canon" in the church. Some doubts were raised concerning a few of these books including Hebrews, James, 2 Peter, 2 and 3 John, Jude, and Revelation. These books lacked universal endorsement. It was not until the fourth century that the disputes were ended and the formal sanction of the entire New Testament Canon was completed. Athanasius of Alexandria cited all 27 books in 367 A.D. In 363

The Council of Laodicea listed all of the present books except Revelation. The Third Council of Carthage in 397 A.D. included all of the present books in the Canon.

During the debates in the early centuries certain criteria emerged by which books were determined to be Canonical. These *notae canonicitatis* included (1) apostolic origin, (2) reception by the original churches, and (3) consistency with the undisputed core of canonical books. Apostolic origin included not only the books that were written by the apostles themselves but also those books that were authorized by the apostles. For example, the Gospel of Mark was seen as carrying the imprimatur of Peter, and the Gospel of Luke the sanction of Paul.

The reception of books by the original churches referred to the cultic use of these writings in the worship and teaching of the churches. The Latin word *recipere* was used in the Muratorian Canon to indicate that the church "received" the New Testament books.[3] Books that were excluded from the canon included such writings as the Didache, the Shepherd of Hermas, the Epistle of Barnabas and First Clement. A study of these books quickly reveals their sub-canonical status. There is a clear recognition, for example, in the writings of Clement that a line exists between apostolic and sub-apostolic authority.

E. F. Harrison writes concerning these sub-canonical books:

> H. E. W. Turner notes that a measure of conflict might arise in the application of these criteria. A book might be widely received and appreciated and yet turn out to be unapostolic. Such was the case with the *Shepherd of Hermas,* which had to be excluded from use in public worship, but which was countenanced for purposes of private edification. This helps to explain the origin of a class of early Christian literature known as ecclesiastical, distinguished alike from canonical and from spurious writings, containing such works as the *Epistle of Clement* and the *Epistle of Barnabas,* as well as the *Shepherd of Hermas.*[4]

In addition to these books the church rejected a rash of spurious books that appeared as early as the second century known as apocryphal books. These books were often linked with the writings of the gnostic heretics who sought to usurp the authority that was vested in the New Testament apostles. The gnostics claimed to have a special elite knowledge (*gnosis*) that transcended the knowledge imparted by the apostles. At the same time they tried to gain apostolic credibility for their books by claiming they were written by the apostles themselves. This was an example of propaganda literature that sought to undermine the apostolic tradition. Origen said of these writings:

> The church receives only four gospels; heretics have many, such as the gospel of the Egyptians, the Gospel of Thomas, etc. These we read, that we may not seem to be ignorant to those who think they know something extraordinary, if they are acquainted with those things which are recorded in these books. Ambrose is credited with saying, "we read these that they may not seem ignorant; we read them, not that we receive them, but that we may reject them; and may know what those things are, of which they make such a boast."[5]

The so-called apocryphal gospels abound with fanciful stories and heretical teaching. Some attempt to fill in details of the childhood years of Jesus. The Gospel of Thomas, for example, contains an account of frivolous miracles performed by the boy Jesus such as fashioning birds out of clay and then making them fly away.

The Old Testament Canon

The chief difference between the Roman Catholic canon and the Protestant canon is found with respect to the inclusion of the Old Testament Apocrypha. The Apocrypha (not to be confused with New Testament apocryphal writings) refers to a series of books composed during the Intertestamental period. The Roman Catholic Church includes the Apocrypha and historic Protestantism excludes it. The Hebrew Scriptures are customarily referred to as "The Law, the Prophets, and the Writings." The issue focuses on the historical question of the extent of the Old Testament canon. Did the Jewish Canon include the Apocrypha?

Frequently reference is made to the difference between the Palestinian Canon and the Alex-andrian Canon. History indicates that the Canon of Hellenized Jews of Alexandria included the Apocrypha but that the Hebrew Bible of the Palestinian Canon excluded it. R. K. Harrison writes:

> In any discussion of the Old Testament canon it is of importance to distinguish between that of the Hebrew Bible and its counterpart in other versions of Scripture. The degree of difference in the idea of a

canon of sacred writings can be seen by
reference on the one hand to the Samari-
tan version, in which only the Pentateuch
was accorded canonicity, and on the other
to the LXX, which included the writings
known as the Apocrypha.[6]

The debate over the question of the
Apocrypha is complex and ongoing. Some have
argued that even in the Alexandrian canon the
Apocrypha was accorded secondary status and
was regarded as "Deutero-canonical." This view
is disputed by Roman Catholic scholars who argue that the Apocrypha belonged to the original
Jewish canon.

The Reformers excluded the Apocrypha because they were persuaded that it did not belong
to the Hebrew canon recognized in Jesus' day.
Turretin remarks:

The Jewish church, to which the oracles of
God were committed (Rom. 3:2), never considered them as canonical, but held the
same canon with us (as admitted by
Josephus, *Against Apion*,. . . . They are
never quoted as canonical by Christ and
the apostles like the others. And Christ, by
dividing all the books of the Old Testament
into three classes (the law, the Psalms and
the prophets), clearly approves of the
canon of the Jews and excludes from it

those books which are not embraced in
these classes. The Christian church for
four hundred years recognized with us the
same and no other canonical books.... The
authors were neither prophets and inspired men, since they wrote after Malachi
(the last of the prophets); nor were their
books written in the Hebrew language (as
those of the Old Testament), but in Greek.
Hence Josephus acknowledges that those
things which were written by his people after the time of Artaxerxes were not equally
credible and authoritative with those which
preceded "on account of there not being an
indisputable succession of prophets."[7]

Church and Canon

One of the great controversies of the
Reformation centered on the relative authority of
church and Scripture. It is often said that
though *Sola Fide* was the material cause of the
Reformation, *Sola Scriptura* was its formal cause.
Luther insisted that both popes and church
councils could err. He rested his case for justification on the Scriptures alone. Rome countered
by arguing that in a real sense the Scripture
owed its authority to the authority of the church
because it was the church who "created" the

canon. This view was sharply criticized by Calvin:

> Nothing, therefore, can be more absurd than the fiction, that the power of judging Scripture is in the church, and that on her nod its certainty depends. When the church receives it, and gives it the stamp of her authority, she does not make that authentic which was otherwise doubtful or controverted, but acknowledging it as the truth of God, she as in duty bound, shows her reverence by an unhesitating assent. As to the question, How shall we be persuaded that it came from God without recurring to a decree of the Church? It is just the same as if it were asked, How shall we learn to distinguish light from darkness, white from black, sweet from bitter? Scripture bears upon the face of it as clear evidence of its truth, as white and black do of their color, sweet and bitter of their taste.[8]

For Calvin the Bible is objectively the Word of God and derives its authority from Him and not from the church. The church does not create Scripture but receives it (*recipimus*) and submits to an authority that is already there. Calvin knew nothing of a Bible that only "becomes" the Word of God after a church declaration or even after the Holy Spirit illumines it.

For the Reformers the Bible was "canon" as soon as it was written. The Word of God has inherent authority. The church is obliged to acknowledge that authority and to submit to it.

The Problem of Canon Reduction

The problem of canon reduction may manifest itself either in crude and blatant terms or in refined and subtle ways. The ancient heretic Marcion represented the crude form of such reduction by rejecting those portions of the New Testament that referred to the God of the Old Testament in a positive light. Marcion's antipathy to Yahweh controlled his selection of books to be included in his abridged version of the New Testament.

More modern forms of canon reduction are more refined and sometimes subtle. This form achieves a similar purpose by providing a canon within a canon. Since Albert Schweitzer's epic work *The Quest for the Historical Jesus*, many subsequent attempts have been made to get to the "real" history of Jesus that underlies the work of the New Testament. The present form of the New Testament is viewed as the creation of the early church with redactions by editors who embellished the narrative history of Jesus. This attempt to watch the grass grow from a distance of nearly two thousand years reaches its nadir in the contemporary work of the "Jesus Seminar."

Perhaps the most important work of canon reduction in the twentieth century was that undertaken by Rudolf Bultmann. Bultmann's program of "demythologizing" the New Testament was an attempt to rid the New Testament of its mythological husk to penetrate to the kernel of truth that is concealed by the husk. It was an attempt to reconstruct the original history as extrapolated from the Kerygma. Bultmann declared:

> All this is the language of mythology, and the origin of the various themes can be easily traced in the contemporary mythology of Jewish Apocalyptic and in the redemption myths of Gnosticism. To this extent *the kerygma is incredible to modern man, for he is convinced that the mythical view of the world is obsolete.* We are therefore bound to ask whether, when we preach the Gospel today, we expect our converts to accept not only the Gospel message, but also the mythical view of the world in which it is set. If not, does the New Testament embody a truth which is quite independent of its mythical setting? If

it does, theology must undertake the task
of stripping the Kerygma from its mythical
framework, of "demythologizing" it.[9]

Bultmann sets forth the task of freeing the
timeless Gospel from a time-bound mythical
framework. He sought a theology of timeless-
ness, a theology that would be relevant to the *hic
et nunc.* He offers us a "here and now" canon,
which reduces the original canon by the radical
critical method of scissors and paste. For the
Gospel to be relevant for modern man the interpreter must come to the text with a "prior understanding," a certain *Vorverstandnis*, which
Bultmann conveniently discovered in the philosophy of Martin Heidegger.

For modern persons to discover anything
meaningful for faith they must come to the text
of Scripture asking the right questions. These
questions are formed by the insights grasped via
existential philosophy. For Bultmann, salvation
is not tied to the strata of history but is punctil-
iar. It occurs not on the horizontal plane of time
and space but comes to us in a moment of decision, vertically from above.

In this schema the Gospel must be rescued
from the three-storied universe of the biblical
world view, which features an earth that is situ-
ated beneath the heaven above and hell below.

He writes:

> *Man's knowledge and mastery of the world*
> have advanced to such an extent through
> science and technology that it is no longer
> possible for anyone seriously to hold the
> New Testament view of the world–in fact,
> there is no one who does. What meaning,
> for instance, can we attach to such phrases
> in the creed as "descended into hell" or
> "ascended into heaven"?. . . It is impossible
> to use electric light and the wireless and to
> avail ourselves of modern medical and sur-
> gical discoveries, and at the same time to
> believe in the New Testament world of
> spirits and miracles. We may think we can
> manage it in our own lives, but to expect
> others to do so is to make the Christian
> faith unintelligible and unacceptable to the
> modern world.[10]

Here we find canon reduction with a
vengeance. G. C. Berkouwer once remarked
about Bultmann's view that theology could sink
no lower. This sanguine view of the matter reveals that Berkouwer was reading history
through rose-colored glasses. He made this re-
mark before the Death of God movement in theology and the more recent Jesus Seminar
wherein biblical criticism degenerated into biblical vandalism.

This shift in focus manifest in Bultmann displays a shift in attention to the matter of Canon from the authenticity of specific books to the question of the authenticity of material within certain books that have been accorded canonical status. Bultmann's program attacked the *formal* nature of the Canon by attacking various forms of literature found within the historic Canon.

Normally the issues raised by Higher Criticism are seen as being chiefly issues of hermeneutics and not about Canon. But the new hermeneutics are rife with implications for the Canon. The Canon is effectively reduced not by subtracting books of the Bible from a designated list but by excising the content of Scripture by a stroke of the hermeneutical pen. The hermeneutics of the Reformation featured the normative principle of grammatico-historical exegesis. But once the content of Scripture was wrenched out of its historical framework this norm was devastated.

The Reformed hermeneutic represented a commitment to seeking the "objective" meaning of the historical text. Bultmann eschewed this methodology arguing that objective interpretation of the Bible was not only not possible, but more importantly, not even desirable. From his vantage point all an objective reading of Scripture would gain us would be a Gospel tied to an irrelevant mythological world view.

The crisis of Canon today is a crisis of world view. It is the result of an ongoing struggle between naturalism and supernaturalism. The modern hermeneutic is an attempt to recover a naturalistic Canon from the supernaturally conceived message of Scripture. All that smacks of anything supernatural is ruled out from the start. The new "Canon" is the rigid Canon of naturalism. Brunner was correct when he observed early on that the real issue we face in this debate is a crisis of unbelief. Bultmannianism and post-Bultmannian theology are a monument to such unbelief where the "Christ of Faith" has little to do with the Christ of history or the Christ of the New Testament.

Evangelical circles have not escaped modern forms of reductionism. The inerrancy controversy of the twentieth century was not merely a war between modernism and fundamentalism or between liberalism and orthodoxy. It cut to the core of professed Evangelicalism itself as professing evangelicals were sharply divided on the question.

A form of canon reduction arose within the ranks of evangelicals in sometimes subtle ways.

Concepts of "limited inerrancy" and the "organic view of Scripture" effected a reduction in the normative function of Scripture. For example, the historic claim that the Sacred Scriptures are the "only infallible rule of faith and practice" underwent a subtle change in some quarters. The new expression was articulated by the formula: "The Bible is infallible only in matters of faith and practice." These formulae sound very much the same but mean two quite different things. To discriminate between them let us examine them more closely:

Premise A: The Bible is the only infallible rule of faith and practice.

Premise B: The Bible is infallible only in matters of faith and practice.

In Premise A the term "only" is restrictive with respect to norms. It declares that there is only one norm or rule that is infallible, namely the Bible. This indicates that the Bible as a whole and in all of its parts is an infallible rule or norm.

In Premise B the term "only" is restrictive in quite a different sense. Here what is restricted is the scope of infallibility within the Bible. That is, only part of the Bible is infallible, namely that part of the Bible that speaks of matters regarding faith and practice. Here we have a Canon that is reduced to that content of Scripture that deals with matters of doctrine and ethics. When the Bible speaks of other matters, such as history, for example, it may be fallible. This of course has a huge impact on the doctrines themselves, but that is often overlooked.

The second critical difference in these two formulae may be seen in their use of the phrase "faith and practice." In Premise A the phrase "faith and practice" defines and delineates the life of the Christian and the life of the church. What else does the Christian or the church have besides faith and practice? Here faith and practice refer to the sum of Christian living. Premise A then means that we have a single infallible rule, which rule governs all of our life.

The function of the phrase "faith and practice" is quite different in Premise B. Here faith and life are limits of the scope of biblical rule. It restricts biblical infallibility to certain portions of the Scripture that speak to faith and practice, thereby reducing the scope of canonical rule.

Canon Addition

The Canon of Scripture is capable not only of being reduced but also of being augmented. A crass form of that would be accomplished simply by adding books to the list of canonical Scriptures. There are few if any people who are lobbying to add contemporary writings to the New Testament. Nevertheless we are living in a time in which countless claims of new revelations are being made. Neo-Pentecostal theology often views messages delivered in tongues or the utterance of "prophecy" as new forms of revelation. Sometimes these revelations are described as true revelations but not necessarily normative for the church (despite their often containing information that might benefit the entire church). If indeed these are new revelations that have value to the church, we ask, why wouldn't they be added to the Canon?

The claims of private new revelations are many. Pat Robertson routinely gets the "word of knowledge" on national television. God reveals specific illnesses of people who live in various parts of the nation as he prays. I have seen him say things like, "Someone in Topeka, Kansas is right this moment being healed of a goiter." This is an astonishing thing. Here is a man hundreds of miles from the scene who is getting supernatural revelation of the healing of a specific disease in a specific city. What puzzles me is the restricted specificity of these revelations. The disease and the city are named, but never the name and address of the person being healed. Here the prophecy can be neither verified nor falsified.

Oral Roberts tells the nation that God has revealed to him that his life will be taken if he doesn't receive a large amount of money in donations. Robert Tilton promises his constituents that He will mail them a special message from God if they send in their donations. These, of course, are crude forms of modern claims to added revelation. How these claims are entertained by the credulous is a matter of consternation for me.

But it gets more subtle. We hear respected Christian leaders claiming that God has "spoken to them" and given specific guidance and instructions upon which they are duty-bound to act and obey. They are careful to note that this divine speech was not in audible form and there is a disclaimer that this is not a new "revelation." Yet the message which is "laid on the heart" is so clear and powerful that to disobey it is to disobey the voice of God. I am not speaking here of the work of the Holy Spirit by which He illumines the text of Scripture in such a sharp manner as to bring us under conviction or direct our paths. But here the Spirit works *in* the Word and *through* the Word. I am speaking of the speaking of the Spirit that men claim is working *apart* from the Word and in *addition* to the Word.

Though such claims are more often than not attended by the disclaimer that they are not revelation, the way they *function* is as revelation so that the distinction between them and *bona fide* revelation is, in actuality, a distinction without a difference.

The true Canon of Scripture is the rule of God that contains the whole counsel of God, nothing less and nothing more. When we subtract from that counsel we are guilty of Canon reductionism. Perhaps the most common practical subtraction in our time within the evangelical community is the subtraction of the Old Testament in general and the Law of God in particular. The Reformation union of Law and Gospel has all but been destroyed in modern Evangelicalism. Luther and Calvin were not Neonomians who sought to construct a novel form of legalism. They were fierce opponents of both legalism and antinomianism. They believed firmly, however, that all of Scripture is revelatory. In one sense the Reformation witnessed a rediscovery of the Old Testament. The Old Testa-ment reveals the character of God. Though Calvin, for example, argued that certain portions of the Old Testament have been abrogated by their perfect fulfillment in Christ, nevertheless the Law still has a salutary role to play in the Christian's life. Calvin's famous threefold use of the Law defended this thesis.

Perhaps we are living in the most antinomian period in church history. It is a time when attention to the Law of God is not considered all that important. This represents a pernicious form of Canon reductionism. The very rule of God Himself is removed from our consideration by it.

Canon and Providence

Though these are perilous times for the church with regard to the normative function of the Bible in our lives, we remain optimistic for the future. That optimism is grounded in our conviction of the providence of God. It was by His singular providence that the Bible was originally given under His superintendence and by His inspiration. It was also by His providence that the original books of the Bible were preserved and accorded the status of Canon. It is in Providence that we trust for the future of the church. The Westminster Confession declares:

> As the providence of God doth, in general, reach to all creatures; so, after a most special manner, it taketh care of his church, and disposeth all things to the good thereof (V:VII).

That the Canon was originally established by a historical selection process, undertaken by fallible human beings and fallible institutions, is no reason to exclude from our consideration the role of the providence of God in these affairs. Some in the Reformed tradition have pointed to a *providentia specialissima* (special providence) in this regard. Abraham Kuyper particularly referred to our ability to trace the course of providence in the establishment of the Canon.[11] It is the invisible hand of Providence in the history of the church along with the explicit promises of Scripture regarding the church and God's own Word that gives comfort to our souls as we rest in the confidence of the abiding work of that same Providence.

1 Benjamin Breckinridge Warfield, *Revelation and Inspiration* (Grand Rapids: Baker, 1927) p. 451.

2 Ibid., p. 455.

3 G.C. Berkouwer, *De Heilige Schrift I* (Kampen: J. H. Kok, 1966) p. 89.

4 Everett F. Harrison, *Introduction to the New Testament* (Grand Rapids.: Eerdmans, 1964) p. 112.

5 Ibid., p. 122.

6 R. K. Harrison, *Introduction to the Old Testament* (Grand Rapids.: Eerdmans, 1969) p. 262.

7 Francis Turretin, *Institutes of Elenctic Theology* Vol. 1, trans. George Musgrave Giger, ed. James T. Dennison, Jr. (Phillipsburg.: P & R, 1992) p. 102.

8 John Calvin, *Institutes of the Christian Religion* Vol. 1, trans. Henry Beveridge (Grand Rapids: Eerdmans, 1969) p. 69.

9 Rudolf Bultmann, *Kerygma and Myth* (New York: Harper & Row, 1961) p. 3.

10 Ibid., pp. 4–5.

11 Berkouwer, *De Heilige Schrift I,* p. 93.

4

The Authority of Scripture

Dr. John H. Armstrong

The Bible has a lot to say about its own authority. A whole lot. Indeed, "The authority of the Scriptures is the great presupposition of the whole of the biblical preaching and doctrine."[1]

It is the constant claim of the writers of Holy Writ that what they write is the authoritative and living Word of God. When the Old Testament is quoted in the New, statements like "God says" and "the Holy Spirit says" are frequent (e.g. Acts 1:16; 3:24, 25; 2 Corinthians 6:16). What "the Scripture says" and what "God says" are quite simply the same thing in case after case. The Scripture is even personified, as if it were God (cf. Galatians 3:8; Romans 9:17). It was B. B. Warfield who noted accurately that the writers of the New Testament could speak of the Scripture doing exactly what Scripture records Jehovah as doing. "And this naturally implies authority," adds Ridderbos.[2] The phrase "It is written" (*gegraptai*), used often in the New Testament, settles the matter beyond reasonable doubt.

When we come to the New Testament writings we immediately note that nothing less than the authority of the Old Testament Scriptures is ascribed to the writers of the New Testament (cf. Romans 1:15; 1 Timothy 2:7; Galatians 1:8, 9; 1 Thessalonians 2:13). *Gegraptai* is used of New Testament writings and the apostolic text is placed on a par with the writings of the Old Testament (cf. 2 Peter 3:15, 16; Revelation 1:3). The concept of faith found in the New Testament is consistent with this witness, for faith is simply obedience to the witness of the apostles, i.e. the New Testament Scripture (cf. Romans 1:5; 16:26; 10:3). We should note:

> This apostolic witness is fundamentally distinguished in this respect from other manifestations of the Spirit, which demand of the congregation (ekklesia) not only obedience, but also a critical discernment between the true and the false (cf. 1 Thess. 5:21; 1 John 4:1). For this witness deserves unconditional faith and obedience, in its written as well as in its oral form.[3]

The authority of the Scripture, then, is not located in human brilliance or witness. It is not

found in the person of Moses, Paul, or Peter. The
authority is found in the sovereign God Himself.
The God who "breathed out"[4] the words through
human writers stands behind every statement,
every doctrine, every promise and every command written in the Scripture. After all, it was
"In the past [that] God spoke to our forefathers
through the prophets at many times and in various ways" (Hebrews 1:1).

Further, the apostle Paul makes a statement
so bold that it must shock us if we carefully
read it. To the church at Corinth he says, "what
I am writing to you is the Lord's command" (1
Corinthians 14:37). His authority, as a writer of
God-breathed Scripture, is *above* all other authority. Why? Because he is an apostle, which,
as we shall soon see clearly, is one specially
commissioned by the Lord to lay the foundation
for the Christian church (cf. Ephesians 2:20;
Revelation 21:2, 14). He was a special representative of the Lord Himself. His word, therefore,
was the very commandment of the Lord![5]

To the authority of this Word all must submit, without rebellion or reservation. Why?
Because this Word has an authority of the most
distinct sort. It has its origin in God's will, not
man's. And it is both complete and final (cf.
Hebrews 1:2, "in these last days He has spoken

to us by His Son"). Of this authority Paul writes:

> The weapons we fight with are not the
> weapons of the world. On the contrary,
> they have divine power to demolish
> strongholds. We demolish arguments and
> every pretension that sets itself up against
> the knowledge of God, and we take captive
> every thought to make it obedient to
> Christ. And we are ready to punish every
> act of disobedience, once your obedience is
> complete (2 Corinthians 10:3–6).

Lutheran theologian Edward W. A. Koehler, writing earlier in our century, correctly concludes that "It [i.e., this authority which comes to us from the Bible itself] calls for instant and unqualified acceptance of every statement of the Bible on the part of man."[6]

Our Lord Jesus, in establishing His own authority during His incarnate earthly ministry, grounded His ultimate judgment in His spoken word which will judge men in the final day. This is true precisely because His word is the very Word of God itself, with all of the authority of Jehovah behind it. He said:

> As for the person who hears my words but
> does not keep them, I do not judge him.
> For I did not come into the world to judge

the world, but to save it. There is a judge
for the one who rejects me and does not accept my words; that very word which I
spoke will condemn him at the last day. For
I did not speak of my own accord, but the
Father who sent me commanded me what to
say and how to say it. I know that his
command leads to eternal life. So whatever
I say is just what the Father has told me to
say (John 12:47–50).

John R. W. Stott has correctly noted that submission to Christ's authority as Lord is "the only
possible attitude of mind in which to approach
our study of Jesus Christ and the authority of
the Word of God." Stott adds that ".belief in the
authority of Scripture and submission to the
authority of Scripture are necessary conse-
quences of our submission to the lordship of
Jesus."[7]

Koehler concludes, "To ignore, disregard, or
reject any doctrine of the Bible is rebellion
against God's authority, and will not go unpun-
ished."[8]

But What Is Meant By "Authority"?

In general the concept of authority is a rela-
tional idea. It is a word which signifies superior-
ity, or dominance. It has been properly said that:

> To have authority is to have a right to rule
> and a claim to exercise control. Authority is
> expressed in directives and acknowledged
> by compliance and conformity. The word
> "authority" is used both abstractly for the
> commanding quality that authoritative
> claims have, and also concretely for the
> source or sources of those claims—"the au-
> thority" or "the authorities." In both us-
> ages the thought of rightful dominance re-
> mains central. [9]

The idea of authority appears regularly in
ordinary conversation. We speak of scholars as
"authorities," meaning those who use original
documents, sources, etc.; or we speak of umpires
in a baseball game as those having "authority"
because they enforce the rules of the game. Law-
makers have authority to make laws while
judges exercise an authority inherent in the laws
themselves.

The Christian conception of authority, however, is quite different from these concepts. Here
we encounter a divine authority, an authority
inherent in the triune God Himself—Father, Son
and Holy Spirit. This is revealed authority precisely because it has been given to us, finally
and completely, in the Word of God. The Word
of God is authoritative precisely because it is
God's verbalized communication to His rational

thinking creatures. It is

> verbalized in both the indicative and the
> imperative moods, and particularized in
> relation to each person to whom it is sent.
> The nearest human analogies to this are the
> authority of legislation enacted by an abso-
> lute ruler, and of orders issued by a
> supreme military commander, for in both
> these cases what is uttered is at the same
> time what the person in authority said (on
> the occasion when the laws or orders were
> first given) and also what he says in the
> present moment since his laws, or orders,
> continue to apply to everyone who stands
> under his authority here and now.[10]

This concept of a distinctly Christian authority is not merely the creation of imaginative theological minds. It can be seen in the longest
chapter in the Scripture, Psalm 119, where all
176 verses excepting one "speak explicitly or
implicitly of due response to what the Psalmist
variously calls God's word, words, precepts,
statutes, law, promise, testimonies and ordinances, which spell out his ways and his righteousness, that is, his revealed will for mankind."[11]

How the authority of this Word comes to us
in our time, how its message is to be discovered

and understood, and in what way human opinions relate to this written Word are all questions
that bear upon this larger question of God's authority. All that I am asserting at the outset of
this chapter is a simple, but very necessary,
fact—what is final authority for a Christian
must be the Word of God which comes from the
Creator as the binding word of His covenant.
That God must, of necessity, as Creator and
sovereign, have authority over all His creatures
is a given. The real debate among those who
profess allegiance to Christ as Lord is not over
the concept of authority itself. For Christians the
debate is over how to regard His authority because He is Lord over all.

Our question is this: "How shall we who
have come to embrace God's authority bend our
wills and lives, explicitly, to this authority which
is God's?" Or more directly related to what we
shall see in this chapter, "What role do human
opinions, or creeds, councils, and church authorities, have in this matter of the authority of
Scripture?" There is agreement, among all Christian traditions, that God has revealed Himself in
the person and work of Jesus Christ. This living
Word is "the way, the truth and the life" (John
14:6). But exactly *how* does Christ make known
to His people the will of the Father? This is the

question which must now concern us.

The Basis of Authority

As previously noted, Scripture openly claims authority for itself. It does this in several ways. The repeatedly-used statement "It is written" (46 times in Scripture, 33 in the New Testament alone) plainly asserts an authority for written Scripture. In addition, we note the frequent use of the phrase "Scripture says" (seven times) and the phrase "according to the Scriptures" (three times), both indicating that an unqualified authority is located in the written text itself. In addition, we have repeated appeals by Jesus to "the law and the prophets" (38 times; e.g., Luke 24: 44–47, a classic example).

Indeed, the frequently used statement "according to the Scriptures" is a most significant clue to the ministry, death, burial and resurrection of Jesus. The epistles are not written as mere expressions of human opinion—albeit important religious opinion—but as an authoritative rule or canon for both doctrine and practice (e.g. 2 Peter 3:2, 16; 1 Timothy 5:8; 2 Thessalonians 3:6). Furthermore, Revelation 22:18–19 concludes the canon with the strongest warning imaginable. Any who would treat the words of this Apocalypse (and it is possible that the whole of Scripture is in view) as something other than the very Word of God, with all the authority inherent in such a statement, is in danger of eternal judgment.

Over the centuries both theologians and the faithful church in general have accepted the authority of Scripture as God's authority. Even when other authorities are put forward this stress is still present, at least initially. As in all ages, still today, new authorities (visions, prophecies, signs from heaven, etc.) are almost always put forward as subservient to the Scripture, even by those who endorse them.

St. Augustine stated this well when he wrote, "In those teachings which are clearly based on Scripture are found *all* that concerns faith and the conduct of life" (emphasis mine). It was this same Augustine who said, "What Scripture says, God says!"

We must further see that the authority claimed for the Bible is not merely a *historical* authority, although this kind of authority *is* claimed for the Scriptures. Consider for a moment this simple fact—almost all that you know about God's redemptive work under the Old Covenant, as well as what you know about the life and ministry of the Lord Jesus, is given in the Scriptures. Further, though we often hear discussion about the "early church" and its beliefs, the only things we really know about the very *first* Christians and the *first* church are *virtually* all contained in the pages of sacred Scripture. These writings are not only primary for our historical knowledge of the Christ, but virtually exclusive. Their historical authority can be seen in the peculiar way in which they speak as firsthand sources and as eyewitness accounts of the events set before them. To put this simply: What would we know of Jesus of Nazareth without the New Testament? Frankly, very little!

This historical authority, as original source material, is surely very important. I do not believe we can make too much of it. But many ancient documents make similar claims and as such are the primary sources for information about men and religious movements. What makes the Scripture unique? These writings describe events in a way that specifically demands the reader to believe in a certain way and to live accordingly. The Bible is, simply put, our *sole* testimony to God's words and great redemptive actions. The Bible does more than pass on historically authoritative information; consistently it has the stubborn habit of making authoritative demands upon our belief and practice.

All of historic Christendom—Roman Catholic, Protestant and Orthodox—is agreed up to this point: Scripture is the Word of God, and as such, it has God's authority! *Vox Scriptura, vox Dei*; "the voice of Scripture is the voice of God." Scripture's authority is ultimately and finally God's authority.

Other Authorities?

Scripture's unique authority has been almost universally accepted by the historic Christian Church. But the nub of the debate for varying Christian traditions has come down to this: *other* authorities have been advanced which, at least in principle, rival or qualify the authority of Scripture. How are we to deal with these *other* authorities?

It is important that we understand several prominent authorities that have been advanced alongside of Scripture.

1. *Oral Tradition.* Note the authority of oral tradition. The argument is quite simple. What is written in Scripture was first spoken. Because it was first spoken it is a living word in a spoken form, and only later does it become inscripturated or written. This oral tradition has a status equal to the written word, since teachings

and practices not written down had authority in the early church. If things not written down had status equal to the Scriptures, then they must still do so in our time as well.

The chronological priority of the spoken word is not in dispute. This is fact. I would even agree that, to the best of our knowledge, Jesus never actually wrote Scripture. But this really begs the important question at hand.

Oral transmission is far more subject to change, deviation and corruption than written communication. With written manuscripts (e.g. as in the study of Scripture) we can compare texts and various manuscripts and families of manuscripts, all the time seeking to get back to the source itself. This simply could not be done for long with oral communication.

Oral communication needed a standard, a North Star, a clear point of reference. The written Scripture alone supplied that point. What is proclaimed orally since the apostolic era is good in itself. It may even have the ring of antiquity about it. But it does not have *ultimate*, or necessary, authority. Why? Because it cannot be heeded in the same way Scripture can be. Peter states this well when he writes in sacred Scripture:

> And we have the word of the prophets
> made more certain, and you will do well to
> pay attention to it, as to a light shining in a
> dark place, until the day dawns and the
> morning star rises in your hearts. Above
> all, you must understand that no prophecy
> of Scripture came about by the prophet's
> own interpretation. For prophecy never
> had its origin in the will of man, but men
> spoke from God as they were carried along
> by the Holy Spirit (2 Peter 1:19–21).

Only what was spoken by (true) prophets and then inscripturated by God could be carefully pondered and ultimately acknowledged as real and final authority throughout the ages. Men who were truly "carried along by the Holy Spirit" eventually wrote (or had written for them) what put the believer under ultimate compulsion and necessity. Oral communication will always be necessary. Indeed it still is the primary means of bringing particular men and women to the faith. But what determines its validity and authority is that it is clearly grounded in the text of Scripture.

Further, no true advocate of the supreme and final authority of Scripture would assert that the immediate hearers of the preaching of Jesus, or the apostles, were free to pick and choose what they would submit to since they did not receive

it in written form. What is asserted in believing
that Scripture alone has final and full authority
is this: God revealed His Word orally and tem-
porarily through prophets and apostles and
then subsequently through the inscripurated
text.

Oral communication, in this post-apostolic
era, is powerful precisely because it relies so
faithfully on the "more certain" word of Scripture itself. Thus we conclude, with the Apostle,
himself a faithful preacher, "Consequently, faith
comes from hearing the message, and the message is heard *through the word of Christ*" (Romans
10:17).

2. *The Church.* The second authority which ri-
vals Scripture is the church. This argument goes
as follows: The church is itself divinely insti-
tuted (Matthew 16:18–20, where Jesus calls it
"*My* church"), and the church came *before* the
Scripture. Indeed, the preaching and teaching
upon which Scripture itself is based came prior
to the canon of Holy Scripture. The church, it is
argued, gave us the canon of Scripture, and the
church, with its proper disciplinary function in
every age, expounds and interprets the Word of
God.

These arguments, in themselves, are again
correct. What is wrong is to assume that they

prove that the authority of the church is *equal to or greater than the authority of the Scripture itself.* Let me explain more fully.

The mistake in the conclusion drawn from the above theses is one of failure to understand the uniqueness of the apostolate. Exactly who were the apostles? What authority did they possess? Is that authority, on some continuing basis, the foundation for further revelation today? In what way?

The church is described in Ephesians as "God's people and members of God's household, built on the foundation of the apostles and prophets, with Christ Jesus Himself as the chief cornerstone" (2:19b–20). Note that the text does not say the church is built upon Christ, but rather upon the apostles and prophets. Christ is the cornerstone that holds the church together, but the foundation upon which this "holy temple" (vs. 21) is established and upon which believers, like "living stones, are being built into a spiritual house, to be a holy priesthood, offering spiritual sacrifices to God through Jesus Christ" (1 Peter 2:5) is the apostolate.

By definition, foundational matters have to do with those things which are at the beginning. You don't lay repeated foundations for a developing house. The point should be obvious.

Those who teach that we need new apostles,
even secondary ones who will add to the primary work of the first century, are really saying
that we need *new* foundations. This would logi-
cally require a *new* cornerstone for each *new*
foundation. Christ is still building His church
but He is building it stone by precious stone
upon a foundation *already laid* because "this
priest had offered for all time one sacrifice for
sins" (Hebrews 10:12a).

The word *apostolos* is a unique and most descriptive New Testament word. John Stott suggests that the word has a double background—
one ancient and one contemporary. This, he
suggests, helps us to understand the meaning of
the term and why Jesus chose this word to describe the unique role of these foundation
builders.

The ancient background of this word can be
seen in the Old Testament's repeated use of this
idea in reference to the prophets of God who
were "sent" with divine commission to speak for
Yahweh (cf. Exodus 3:10; Numbers 16:28–29;
Isaiah 6:8; Jeremiah 1:7; Ezekiel 2:3; Jeremiah
35:15; where in each of these cases the "sending"
is "not a vague dispatch but a specific commission to assume the role of a prophet and to
speak God's word to the people").[12] When Jesus

used this particular word it is evident that He was likening the men He called to be apostles to Yahweh's prophets during the Old Covenant era.

Stott suggests, further, that there is a contemporary reason for the use of this word by Jesus and the New Testament. *Apostolos* is the Greek equivalent of the Aramaic *shaliach*, which

> already had a well defined meaning as a teacher sent out by the Sanhedrin to instruct the Jews of the Dispersion. As such *shaliach* carried the authority of those he represented, so that it was said, "the one who is sent is as he who sent him." In the same way Jesus sent out his apostles to represent him, to bear his authority and teach in his name, so that he could say of them: "He who receives you receives me" (Mat. 10:40; cf. John. 13:20).[13]

The apostle was a specially chosen emissary, a bearer of higher authority vested in him by God Himself. What this means is that the apostles were *proxies* for their Lord. Prior to Pentecost the twelve are only infrequently referred to as apostles (cf. Matthew 10:1–2; cf. also John's record). They are, as others, more often termed "disciples." But after the resurrection and the gift of the Holy Spirit these unique men became

proxies who stood virtually in the place of
Christ, possessing unique authority. They had
His unique power and His unique teaching (e.g.
2 Corinthians 12:12 which identifies "the things
that mark an apostle—signs, wonders and miracles"). The words of an apostle carried an authority quite unlike the words of a present- day
minister, priest, or Pope. That this is true can be
seen in the way one Apostle writes this exhortation: "I want you to recall the words spoken in
the past by holy prophets and the command
given by our Lord and Savior through your apostles" (2 Peter 3:2).

The apostles were eyewitnesses to the risen
Lord and of necessity each was "a witness . . . of
his resurrection" (Acts 1:22). Paul, a unique
apostle to the Gentiles, was used to establish
even more clearly the gospel and the unique
new covenant. He was an eyewitness to the res-
urrected Lord in a special way. Three times in
the Acts of the Apostles (note the very name of
this fifth book of the canon) Paul testifies to his
having seen the risen Christ on the road to
Damascus. Paul confirmed this on several different occasions (cf. 1 Corinthians 9:1; 15:4–8; 2
Corinthians 10:5).

The words of Jesus in John 16:13 are variously interpreted. What is patently obvious that

the promise that "He will guide you into all truth" is not general but rather a very specific promise that as apostles they would teach (and thus write) the truth and nothing but the truth. Further a correct memory of all He had taught them was promised (cf. John 14:26).

When one reads the statements of early church fathers (i.e., those earliest writings outside the New Testament writings) it becomes immediately evident that these writers considered all they wrote to be built upon a prior and more fundamental authority found in the writings of the apostles. Ignatius, as an example, said, in A.D. 117, that he was not competent to write to the church as though he were an apostle: "I do not, like Peter and Paul, issue commandments unto you. They were apostles."

So the question of canonicity is not one *ultimately* decided by the church either. It is one principally decided by authorship: "Was it written by an apostle or with apostolic approval and involvement (as examples of the latter category we include Mark and James)?" This is the important question. The church never decided which books were inspired and which were authoritative. This had already been decided by the appointment of the apostolate by the risen Lord Himself. The church recognized this fact and properly *received* the canon.

Yes, the church must judge and it does rule. The church has made important decisions through the ages. And we would do well to study these and consider why they were made and what caused them. The authority of the church must never be treated lightly, a thing done by North American Christians in our time. But the church's authority is always to be grounded in a prior, more primary, authority— namely in the writings of the apostles. We conclude then that only when the church speaks biblically is its authority absolute. When the church does not speak according to the Word of God it has lost its light and has itself drifted into the darkness (cf. Isaiah 8:20).

3. *Creeds, Church Councils, and the Fathers.* A third source of challenge to the full and final authority of Scripture has been creeds, confessions, and even the fathers of the early church. It is correct that the church issues official and unofficial pronouncements on moral and doctrinal issues that affect her life in every age. These must be grounded in the Word of God. Such statements, as seen in historic creeds, have a real authority. We do well to read them, to consult them and to carefully understand them. But their authority is never final. It is always *relative*

authority. Most of the work of the historic councils of the church, and much of the thought put
into now-famous confessions, is sound and
good. We are foolish to think, independently as
postmodern people, that we do not need such
historic contributions. But even these are to be
judged by the one absolute, supreme authority.

It is the conviction of the various contributors
to this present volume that the sixteenth-century
Reformation was fundamentally a recovery of the
full and final authority of the Scripture. It provided a correct reply to the numerous challenges
to the authority of Scripture that had arisen over
several centuries.

If the church in our time would wholeheartedly, and with true understanding, return to the
final authority of Scripture she would avoid
numerous problems presently ignored or misunderstood. We would do well to hear the advice of Martin Luther who wrote:

> Jesus . . . subjects the whole world to the
> apostles, through whom alone it should
> and must be enlightened. . . . All the people
> in the world—kings, princes, lords, learned
> men, wise men, holy men—have to sit
> down while the apostles stand up, have to
> let themselves be accused and condemned
> in their wisdom and sanctity as men who
> know neither doctrine nor life nor the right

relation to God.[14]

The Central Argument for the Authority of Scripture

The central argument for the supremely authoritative, uniquely revealed, and verbally inspired Holy Scripture, is not that difficult to grasp. It all leads us back to the *unique* authority of Jesus Himself. It was He who endorsed the Old Testament Scriptures as the Word of God, both in specific statements and in how He used them (e.g., Matthew 5:17–20; 12:18–27; 26:52–54; Luke 10:25–26; 16:17). Further, it was He who foresaw the writing of the New Covenant Scriptures and who made provision for this by appointing the apostles to be His proxies so that they might lay the foundation of the church upon His unique person and work.

But isn't this argument, as some have suggested, circular? Some suggest that evangelical Protestants argue as follows: "Scripture is inspired because the divine Son of God said so, but we know the divine Son of God only through the Scriptures." Such a stereotypical response actually fails to understand the argument and thus misrepresents it seriously.

The argument, as Stott has ably shown, "is not circular but linear."[15] We come to the

Gospels and their story of Jesus and in taking them at face value, as eyewitness accounts, we meet Christ, through the illuminating work of the Holy Spirit. Having met the Christ, who is Lord, we listen to Him and thus discover that this Lord gives us a doctrine of Scripture and its authority. This is not a circular argument, but one that builds on a beginning and then travels in a line from that beginning point. Simply stated we come to "historical documents [which] evoke our faith in Jesus, who then gives us a doctrine of Scripture."[16]

Can you not see that the central issue here relates to Christ Himself?

Authority and the Great Divide

Because Scripture is the Word of God, by virtue of its inspiration it must possess divine properties or divine attributes. These properties include not only its authority, but also its efficacy, perfection, and perspicuity.[17] My purpose presently is to examine the nature of the authority of sacred Scripture more clearly as it relates to these particular properties. Each will be considered in terms of both the teaching of Scripture itself and the historical challenge to each raised by the continued refusal of some

Christian traditions to submit to the *final* authority of God in Scripture alone.

This concern was expressed most clearly in the great debate which took place in the sixteenth century over the doctrine of *sola scriptura*. The Reformers believed that the Roman Catholic church had corrupted the doctrine of the authority of Scripture, and thus had *materially* altered the very foundation of the Christian Church. In reality the Reformation debate regarding the authority of Scripture was not like the debate in our age. The Reformation debate was more directly about *sole* authority; thus the word *sola* was connected with Scripture in the now-famous phrase, *sola Scriptura*. (This, by the way, is why the historic Protestant confessions have little in them about the questions of authority that were later raised in the nineteenth century.) Let us look back at this debate regarding *sole* authority briefly.

Scripture: The Sole Source of Authority

Heinrich Heppe, writing in the last century, refers to Holy Scripture as "the one source and norm of all Christian knowledge."[18] In the words of Jude the faith of the Christian Church is one "given once for all time" (vs. 3). Scripture, as already noted, has unique authority. But why? Because it is primary and unique, not *primus inter pares* ("first among equals"). If it were the latter then it would be a source equal to others in certain ways. But Scripture has no equal precisely because Scripture alone has its source in God, who, by the Holy Spirit, is its Author.

But Scripture also has an authority that is normative. By this I mean that Scripture has an authority which is much more than descriptive. This is precisely the point made by several historic Protestant confessions which state this. Note the following:

> The Church of Christ makes no laws or commandments without God's Word. Hence all human traditions, which are called ecclesiastical commandments, are binding upon us only in so far as they are based on and commanded by God's Word. [19]

> We believe that the Word contained in these books has proceeded from God, and receives its authority from him alone, and not from men. And in as much as it is the rule of all truth, containing all that is necessary for the service of God and for our salvation, it is not lawful for men, nor even for angels, to add to it, or to take away from it, or to change it. Whence it follows that

no authority, whether of antiquity, or cus-
tom, or numbers, or human wisdom, or
judgments, or proclamations, or edicts, or
decrees, or councils, or visions, or miracles,
should be opposed to these Holy Scriptures, but on the contrary, all things
should be examined, regulated, and reformed according to them.[20]

And getting more directly at what has been
called the internal witness of the Spirit, another
confession adds:

We receive these books, and these only, as
holy and confirmation of our faith; believing without any doubt all things contained
in them, not so much because the church
receives and approves them as such, but
more especially because the Holy Ghost
witnesses in our hearts that they are from
God, whereof they carry the evidence in
themselves.[21]

Adding to this, we conclude that to receive
the Scriptures as our sole source and norm for
both faith and practice is to submit to Christ
Himself, as we saw earlier.

Therefore, we do not admit any other judge
than Christ himself, who proclaims by the
Holy Scriptures what is true, what is false,

what is to be followed, or what is to be avoided.[22]

Uniformly, without any equivocation, these sixteenth-century evangelicals elevated the authority of Scripture to a place above all other authority in the church. They did this believing that they were keeping Christ in the place of sole authority over all that pertained to the church. Thus, in a most important way, *solus Christus* (i.e., "Christ alone") was not only linked to *sola fide*, and thus to salvation doctrine, but also to *sola scriptura*, or to the authoritative basis for faith.

The Roman Catholic view, which stands in sharp distinction from that given above, was clearly posited at the Council of Trent. The Council showed that it fundamentally rejected the Reformers' efforts to call the church back to the authority of the Word of God. In the fourth session (April 8, 1546), the Council of Trent said that

> the purity itself of the Gospel be preserved in the Church: which (Gospel) before promised through the prophets in the holy Scriptures, our Lord Jesus Christ, the Son of God, first promulgated with His own mouth, and then commanded to be preached by His Apostles to every crea-

ture, as the fountain of all, both saving truth, and moral discipline; and seeing clearly that this truth and discipline are contained in the written books, and the unwritten traditions, received by the Apostles from the mouth of Christ himself, or from the Apostles themselves, the Holy Spirit dictating, have come down even unto us, transmitted as it were from hand to hand: [the Synod] following the examples of the orthodox Fathers, receives and venerates with an equal affection of piety and reverence, all the books both of the Old and of the New Testament—seeing that one God is the author of both—as also the said traditions, as well those appertaining to faith, as to morals, as having been dictated, either by Christ's own word of mouth, or by the Holy Ghost, and preserved in the Catholic Church by a continuous succession.[23]

It is most important that the reader understand the issue at stake here. It is not, "Is all that Christ taught to be found in Scripture?" (cf. John 20:30). Nor is it, "What is Scripture?" (i.e., the question of canon, or of which books were part of the New Testament). The question is: Should oral traditions, creeds, church fathers, or writings of an extrabiblical sort ever be allowed to stand alongside the Holy Scripture as equal authority? Put in a different way we might ask: What is the supreme court of all appeals to which all matters of faith and practice are directed? The answer of Rome was, and still is, clear. Trent said that "the unwritten traditions, whether referring to faith or to conduct, are to be received with the *same pious feeling* as Scripture" (italics mine). The modern Catholic Church has confessed the same view plainly in the *Catechism of the Catholic Church* (1994) when it says:

> And [Holy] Tradition transmits in its entirety the Word of God which has been entrusted to the apostles by Christ the Lord and the Holy Spirit. . . . As a result the Church, to whom the transmission and interpretation of Revelation is entrusted, does not derive her certainty about all revealed truths from the Holy Scripture alone. Both Scripture and Tradition must be accepted and honored with equal sentiments of devotion and reverence. ("The Relation Between Tradition and Sacred Scripture," Part One, II, p. 26).

Certain Catholic apologists have referred to explicit and implicit authority. By this they mean to say that Scripture is insufficient in a direct sense, needing supplement through the church's interpretive role. (This can be seen in the above quotation from the modern Catechism.) Only, then, in a *limited* sense can one speak of authority and sufficiency in the Scripture.

Protestant apologists have been historically quick to counter by insisting that Scripture alone is to be *canon et regula fidei* (i.e., "the canon and rule of faith"), because a rule which is insufficient, or incomplete and not final, is really no rule at all. Turretin, a Reformed scholar of the seventeenth century, argued that as the New Testament is Christ's final will and testament, and since no one dare add to a deceased person's will, then how dare one add to Christ's divine will (cf. Galatians 3:15)? Only with a *supreme, final and sufficient* authority can the church itself have anything which is reliable, internally consistent, and never misleading. That authority has to be in Scripture alone.

This Divine Authority Observed

1. *Divine Authority and Witness of the Spirit.* But how does Scripture actually *become* divine authority for us? Christian certainty (*fides divina*) is created solely by the self-testimony of the Word of God, through the power of the Holy Spirit op-

erating in it, not through the employment of human proofs. This is the obvious meaning of 1 Corinthians 2:4–5: "My message and my preaching were not with wise and persuasive words, but with a demonstration of the Spirit's power, so that your faith might not rest on men's wisdom, but on God's power." Jesus taught the same when He said, "For my Father's will is that everyone who looks to the Son and believes in him [i.e., hears Christ's word and believes savingly in him] shall have eternal life, and I will raise him up at the last day" (John 6:40). And in the next chapter of John, "If anyone chooses to do God's will, he will find out whether my teaching comes from God or whether I speak on my own" (John 7:17). In the words of Lutheran theologian Francis Pieper, "The Word of Scripture, being the Word of God, is an object of perception that creates its own organ of perception, of faith, and thus Scripture itself bears witness to its [own] divine authority."[24]

By this is meant the doctrine of *testimonium Spiritus Sancti internum*, or the so-called internal witness of the Spirit. This witness does not exist simply in the human emotions. It is already present in the Scripture itself and it comes with Spirit-wrought faith in the testimony of the

Scripture. This is the idea inherent in the words
of the apostle who writes:

> We accept man's testimony, but God's tes-
> timony is greater because it is the testi-
> mony of God, which He has given about
> His Son. Anyone who believes in the Son
> of God has this testimony in his heart.
> Anyone who does not believe God has
> made him out to be a liar, because he has
> not believed the testimony God has given
> about his Son (1 John. 5:9, 10).

This internal witness, or testimony, can be
seen in the letter of Paul to the Thessalonians
where he writes:

> And we also thank God continually be-
> cause, when you received the word of God,
> which you heard from us, you accepted it
> not as the word of men, but as it actually is,
> the word of God, which is at work in you
> who believe (1 Thessalonians 2:13).

This is, further, why the Scripture speaks of
faith in the Word of God as a seal, or a confirmation, of God's utter truthfulness (cf. John
3:33). But isn't this a doctrine without *practical*
consequence on the level of true authentication?
Not at all. When we are assailed by doubts regarding the authority of the Scripture what are

we to do? The answer of this truth is that we must have more profound intercourse with the Word of God itself. Here, as we read, meditate, and study the Scripture we are acted upon by God the Holy Spirit who bears witness to the supreme authority of the Word through the self-testimony of the Scripture.

Rome objects to this doctrine precisely because she continues to set the church and the papacy over the Scriptures. Moderns often seek to drive a wedge here as well, severing faith from the inherent authority of Scripture itself. But it is an observable and common fact that we accept a thing through *perceiving* it. I believe, for example, that the moon shines full on a particular evening because I *perceive* that it does.

Besides *fides divina* we also recognize a *fides humana*, or an argument for the authority of the divine word based on human reason. This argument says: As a natural, rational observation of creation reveals God as its Creator (cf. Romans 1:18ff.), so a rational observation of the teaching of Holy Scripture points to God as its author. When Scripture is compared with other "divine" or "holy" books in the world (e.g., the Koran) we see the astounding power of the Scripture, both in its doctrines and in its effect upon those who hear it. This is the area in

which the more formal work of apologetics occurs (Christ seems to have used such an argument, or apologetic, in Matthew 22:29). Extremes
of either seeing too much in this approach, or
too little, should be carefully avoided. Ultimately,
it must be God's gift of *fides divina*, through the
internal witness of the Holy Spirit, that gives a
person confidence in the Scripture as God's
supreme authority.

It is most important that we understand that
this internal witness of the Spirit is tied directly
to the Gospel itself, i.e., the message of "Christ
and him crucified" (1 Corinthians 1:18–2:5).
One must come to believe, as the Reformers
taught, *satisfactio Christi vicaria*, i.e., in the vicari-
ous satisfaction of Christ's death for him as a
sinner. Without this reality the inner witness of
the Spirit to the truth of Scripture can never be
known. Any witness regarding the Scripture that
does not bring the recipient savingly to the
Gospel, and thus to Christ crucified in my place,
is not the work of the Spirit and will not, therefore, give a person confidence in the authority of
the Holy Scripture.

The witness of the Holy Spirit to the authority of Scripture is present when we are filled
with joy in the richness and power of the truth.
But it is also present when it is not so obviously

felt. The heart may long for and cling to God in the word of Scripture. This is why Luther correctly wrote that "The Spirit is given to no one without and outside the Word; He is given only through the Word."[25]

The situation, then, is this: The Holy Ghost, who originally spoke His Word through the Apostles and prophets, remains united with His Word until Judgment Day. Through His Word the Spirit works that faith which believes on the basis of the Word itself and not on the basis of rational arguments or human authorities. This is Christian, or divine, faith (*fides divina*) in contrast to a mere human opinion, or conviction (*fides humana*).[26]

2. *Divine Authority and Efficacy.* The church has no word of its own. Luther put this correctly when he wrote, "No book teaches anything concerning eternal life except this one alone."[27] By this he meant that if any other book or writing teaches correctly regarding eternal life it does so exactly because it is faithful to Scripture.

But in what does this efficacy consist? I answer, in the way it affects man. It does this in ways that exceed all earthly and human power. The Law has power, through the Word of God, to bring the conviction of sin (cf. Romans 3:20). The Gospel has inherent power to work faith in the human heart through the preaching of its truth (cf. Romans 10:17). Pieper is again a helpful instructor to us when he writes:

> The Word of the Gospel, presented in Scripture, has the inherent power to write God's Law into the heart of man, that is, so to change man inwardly that he gladly subjects himself to God's Law and willingly and with delight walks in the ways of God according to the new man, which is created in him through faith in the Gospel. Human strength and human training cannot accomplish this change.[28]

Within the camp of the Protestant Reformers there were differing views on this matter but it seems they all agreed that this divine power never operated outside the Word of God, nor even alongside of it, but rather *through the Word*. Thus, there is an authority inherent in the Word which operates efficaciously *only* through the teaching of Scripture, or, even more literally, through the preaching of Christ (cf. again Romans 10:17).

3. *Divine Authority and Sufficiency*. Is Scripture able to judge between truth and error in all matters of faith and practice? The doctrine of the sole authority of Scripture answers with an unmistakable "yes." Scripture is not an encyclope-

dia of facts pertaining to all areas of human knowledge. There is an area of natural reason and of human experience not addressed by the Word of God.

Further, the Scriptures do not reveal *all* divine truth (1 Corinthians 13:12; Romans 11:33–34). Mystery still is very much a part of our faith in this present age. There is much we do not understand, but Scripture does teach all that we need to know to obtain eternal life and to live to the glory of God (2 Timothy 3:15). Quenstedt, a Lutheran theologian, said this well:

> Holy Scripture is perfect . . . in the sense of a restricted perfection, in so far as it teaches all things that a Christian needs to know in order to believe correctly and to lead a saintly and pious life here on earth.[29]

It is obvious, then, given this perfection of Scriptural authority, that the Word of God does not need to be supplemented by any outside source of doctrine, be it found in tradition, decrees, confessions or in the Pope. Indeed, if this perfection and sufficiency are surrendered the true authority of the Word of God will be surrendered.

What has Rome done in the face of this argument? She has argued that there is a *perfectio implicita Scripturae Sacrae*, i.e., a Scripture which is perfect only when supplemented by the "Church." This means that without the Pope and the magisterium of the church there really is no *completely sufficient* authority to be found in Scripture. In this way of thinking Scripture has been called a *norma remissiva* (a weakened or relaxed norm), but this is no real authority at all.

> According to this notion Scripture would have been sufficient if it had said: "Hear the Church," or rather, according to the Roman interpretation: "Hear the Pope!" But the Pope is not the man of whom Scripture says: "Hear ye Him," Matthew 17:5.[30]

4. *Divine Authority and Perspicuity.* According to Roman Catholic dogma Scripture becomes clear only through the light which shines out through the church itself. According to modern charismatics and enthusiasts of all types Scripture is illumined, or made plain, by a personal or privatized inner light, which is communicated directly or immediately to the soul. According to modern theologies of various sorts the Bible presents a mixture of truth and error and by means of Christian experience the person sorts all this out and clarifies the matter. As has been noted, Reformation theologians saw

one common thread—this all makes man the decisive factor.

Does this doctrine of the clarity of Scripture mean that we find no problems in interpreting the Word of God, no difficulties exegetically, no "hard sayings" in the Word? Of course not. This would be patently absurd. Further, this doctrine does not mean that we need no skills, linguistic or technical, to carefully study the Word of God. (We do need a trained ministry for the edification of the church.)

But having said this we should observe that when Erasmus declared widely how truly obscure the Scriptures were Luther correctly answered him:

> I certainly grant that many passages in the Scriptures are obscure and hard to elucidate, but that is due, not to the exalted nature of their subject, but to our own linguistic and grammatical ignorance; and it does not in any way prevent us knowing all the contents of Scripture. For what solemn truth can the Scriptures still be concealing, now that the seals are broken, the stone rolled away from the door of the tomb, and that greatest of all mysteries brought to light—that Christ, God's Son, became man, that God is Three in One, that Christ suffered for us, and will reign for-

> ever? And are not these things known, and
> sung in our streets? Take Christ from the
> Scriptures—and what more will you find in
> them? You see then, that the entire content
> of the Scriptures has now been brought to
> light, even though some passages will con-
> tain some unknown words that remain ob-
> scure.[31]

Basically, "perspicuity" (or clarity) means the Bible is self-interpreting as to its *essential* truths. This truth seems presupposed, as a matter of course, in Luke 16:29: "They have Moses and the Prophets; let them listen to them." We read, in words that came from the lips of our Lord: "Search the Scriptures" (John 5:39). This counsel would be meaningless unless all readers can know the truth through the Scriptures. Further, the Bereans are commended as the most noble of all early Christians because "They searched the Scriptures daily" to see if the oral teachings of even an apostle were faithful to the text (cf. Acts 17:11). Again, the assumption is that in truly searching the Scriptures truth can be clearly discovered. The fact is, most of the epistles of the New Testament were written to entire congregations to be read in public. If they could not be clearly understood, then the church could not know the directions of the apostle.

But we must go even further than this. Not only is this idea of clarity presupposed by texts such as the above but it is most *plainly* taught by several others. Scripture speaks of itself as "a light shining in a dark place" (2 Peter 1:19) and as "a lamp unto our feet and a light unto our path" (Psalm 119:105). Paul very specifically says to young Timothy that "from infancy you have known the Holy Scriptures" (2 Timothy 3:15) and the Psalmist says that the Word and statutes of God are "making wise the simple" (Psalm 19:7). To attack the perspicuity of Scripture is a not-so-subtle attack upon the very authority of Scripture itself.

But the detractor demurs: "If the Scriptures are so clear the public office of teacher is not *really* needed." I answer, one truth does not exclude the other. We are told by Scripture that we need such teachers in the church (Ephesians 4: 11–12), and the same Scripture teaches us its own clarity. Indeed, those who are taught in the church are told to judge, on the basis of Scripture, if their teachers are true or false prophets. This is to be done on the basis of whether their teachers depart from the Word of the Apostles (cf. Matthew 7:15; Romans 16:17). The institution of teachers for the church actually shows how concerned God is for the well-being of His people. He has gone to great lengths to give light to His people if they will seek Him for it.

Even Luther himself admitted, "It is indeed true some passages in Scripture are obscure."[32] Pieper has stated this matter clearly:

> These obscure passages either do not pertain directly to the Christian doctrine, but give chronological, topographical, archaeological, etc., data, or, if they do pertain to doctrine, the same matter is elsewhere stated in Scripture set forth clearly and explicitly.[33]

And St. Augustine adds, "In the clear passages of Scripture everything is found that pertains to faith and life." And as Luther counsels wisely, "If you cannot understand the obscure, then stay with the clear."[34]

Augustine, indeed, sums up my point well by writing:

> The Holy Ghost has arranged Holy Scripture in such a magnificent and wholesome way that through the clear passages He appeases the hunger and through the dark passages He prevents loathing. For hardly anything is derived from the obscure passages but what is stated elsewhere more clearly.[35]

As we previously demonstrated, the true light of Scripture shines only into the hearts of those given faith by the Holy Spirit (cf. 2 Corinthians 4:1–6). The doctrinal truth of Scripture is plain at one level, but only those regenerated by the Spirit of God will love, embrace and accept the teaching of Scripture as from God. This simply cannot be overstated. What the Holy Spirit works in those who receive the doctrines of the Scripture is true faith, and this is a *specific* faith—it consists of trust in the crucified One, the Lord Jesus Christ.

What Does "Authority" Mean in This Age?

In what ways is the truth of biblical authority challenged in our time? I suggest that authority is being challenged in at least five ways. Let us consider these.

1. *By limiting the nature and scope of inspiration, thus authority.* A famous liberal once said, "It is quite true that the Bible is inspired but so are many other literary treasures of the world." As we have seen, this begs the question of what inspiration actually is. Another more conservative scholar argues that it is "the truths which are inspired but not the words." But what could this possibly mean since the words are the chosen

vehicles for communicating the truths themselves? A fallible "God-breathed" book is a contradiction, a verbal illogicallity.

2. *By restricting the application of Scriptural authority*. To say, as some do, that the Bible is authoritative in matters of faith and conduct and
yet to deny its authority in important areas such
as worship, counseling, mission and music is to
deny its authority. When the Bible speaks, God
speaks. If this is still so then we must learn to
apply the Scripture to all the church as well as
to the believer more directly.

3. *The influence of human philosophy opposes the
authority of Scripture*. The gospel owes nothing to
human wisdom. It is a revelation of God. The
Scripture is not the product of human opinion,
but the opening up of God's thought to us. We
should understand how men think (i.e. philosophy) but we must not force the Word of God to
fit into a human philosophy. We must inten-
tionally allow it to judge our fallen philosophies.

Philosophy seeks after truth. It originates
with man and is always tentative and relative. It
is powerless to save. Scripture proclaims truth.
It is absolute, the final and saving power of God
in Christ. It humbles men before the sovereign
God.

4. *Modern versions of word and faith teaching at-*

tack the authority of the Scripture. "God told me" is bad enough, but now we have special "words of knowledge" which come to modern enthusiasts.

The Reformers had their own versions of this in the sixteenth century. Luther once dealt directly with a group of charismatics ("enthusiasts"). An observer of this meeting wrote:

> He patiently heard the prophet relate his visions; and when the harangue was finished he said, "You mentioned nothing of Scripture." Anabaptist Thomas Muntzer complained, "The doctrine of Luther is not sufficiently spiritual. Divines should . . . acquire a spirit of prophecy, otherwise their knowledge of theology would not be worth one half a penny." Luther added, "You yourself must hear the voice of God," they say." The Bible means nothing. They are not Christians who want to go beyond the Word . . . even if they boast of being full and overfull with ten holy spirits.[36]

Luther once sarcastically noted: "Any teaching which does not square with Scripture is to be rejected even if it snows miracles every day."[37] Calvin added that we should speak only when the Scripture speaks and be silent when Scripture is silent. Wise counsel!

Modern personal words from God repeatedly

set the authority of Scripture on its head. Further, modern proponents of psychotherapeutic reformations need to be rejected as false teachers when they write: "Where the sixteenth-century Reformation returned our focus to the sacred Scriptures as the only infallible rule for faith and practice, the new reformation will return our focus to the sacred right of every person to self-esteem."[38] The result of all of this is, and will continue to be, chaos. "To the law and to the testimony! If they do not speak according to this word, they have no light of dawn" (Isaiah 8:20).

5. *Seriously distorted interpretations challenge the authority of scripture.* What has been called the *analogia fidei*, or "analogy of faith" (e.g., "in proportion to his faith" in Romans 12:6b) is to be observed in the Scriptures. By this is meant that, in the light of the overriding truth of Scripture, all Scripture finds its intended meaning. No one portion of Scripture should be put over against another. This is a principal missing ingredient in much modern exegesis of Scripture.

Luther properly explained this vital truth when he wrote:

> Anyone who ventures to interpret words in the Scriptures any other way than what they say, is under obligation to prove this

> contention out of the text of the very same
> passage or by an article of faith"[39]

Here both Catholic and fundamentalist exegetes often err in strangely similar ways. The authority of ancient church tradition keeps some Catholic exegesis from the plain meaning of many texts, though this has changed among some Catholic scholars in recent years. For many fundamentalists their own man-made traditions, often only a few decades in duration, hinder the plainest word of Scripture from finding the heart. (As an example try engaging many fundamentalists about the subject of regeneration and you will soon discover their mechanical notions will generally prevail over their seriously dealing with the text of John 3.)

Scripture demands interpretation, furthermore, that flows out of what has been called the grammatical-historical method. Here I have in view questions such as: "What was the author's meaning? What is his intention? His audience?" We must do careful research in the text of Scripture using proper historical, linguistic and lexicographical tools. Exegesis, after all, means "to take out of." It never means to add to what is not there. And the Scripture must be interpreted in its literal sense, meaning nouns are nouns, verbs are verbs, and miracles are truly miracles.

R. C. Sproul has correctly suggested that when the unity of Scripture is lost in modern interpretations of the Scripture it becomes something like watching a tennis match without a net between the players.

Further, legalism undermines Scriptural authority in the same manner. Michael Horton has ably shown that whenever we impose moral expectations upon ourselves, or others, which are not clearly and plainly revealed in Scripture we have set up our own norms for the covenant and thereby *trivialized* the authority of Scripture. Let the reader beware!

It is a strange time indeed when believers know more about the Antichrist and the Beast in the Revelation than they do about justification, original sin, election, the cost of true discipleship and eternal judgment. Yet we are told repeatedly that these rather speculative prophetical matters are the "deep truths of the Scripture."

It is also a mark of our lack of reverence for the authority of Scripture that we have thousands of Christians sitting around in small groups asking one another, "What does that passage say to *you*?" I answer, "Who cares what it says to you?" It's as if Bible interpretation has become a matter of multiple choice.

Conclusion

Several important points have emerged in our study. We need to briefly note these in conclusion.

1. Mischief is always the result when rival authorities are set up alongside the Scripture.

If any authority is made coequal to Scripture the normativeness of Scripture's authority is seriously disturbed and the results are seismic. Without an anchor the life of the believer is tossed to and fro in a manner that attacks the foundation laid in Scripture.

2. Conversely, acknowledgment of Scripture's authority actually establishes the proper authority of other sources which will help us mature as believers.

Geoffrey W. Bromiley said well that "the absoluteness of the Bible is not absolutism." When confessions and creeds are seen in their proper place, when the writings of the church fathers are related to Scripture as the final court of appeal, when the church and its public ministry are accountable to Scripture alone, then all of these have a proper place. Their weight, as secondary sources, is important, indeed very important, for here we have earnest and well-trained minds and hearts wrestling with the very authority of the Word itself. To ignore these contributions, secondary though they are, is the height of contemporary arrogance and leads inevitably to independent foolishness. Modern evangelicalism needs to hear this message!

3. The truth that secondary sources have their own authority, albeit under Scripture, is a reminder to all that we are not, ultimately, the judges of truth.

We may rightly ask, "Is this teaching faithful to Scripture?" We must "search the Scriptures" as did the Bereans and we must carefully challenge the teaching of any minister of the Word only with the Word, and that in the right spirit. As Bromiley has properly written,

> Even where we have reason to suspect they might be in error, we must proceed with due caution and respect, recognizing that in the upshot they might still have the best of the argument. Like tradition, the individual Christian is infallible only where he is truly biblical, and he is not always as biblical as he thinks. In reminding him of this the secondary authorities play a role of inestimable value."[40]

Evangelical Bishop Thomas Cranmer centuries ago said, "The Word of God is above the church." So it is. And James I. Packer several years ago added, "The religion in which our Lord was brought up was first and foremost a religion of subjection to the authority of a written divine Word." So it was.

Without the Scripture the believer has no authority for there is no "word of the prophets made more certain" (2 Peter 1:19) without Scripture. With the Scripture the most ordinary and weak Christian has a "God breathed" word that will always be found "useful for teaching, rebuking, correcting and training in righteousness, so that the man of God may be thoroughly equipped for every good work" (2 Timothy 3:16). Such authority will always make both him and his life something to truly be reckoned with in this present age and in the age to come.

---

1. Herman Ridderbos, *Studies in Scripture and its Authority*. (Grand Rapids: Eerdmans, 1978), p. 20.

2. Ibid., p. 21.

3. Ibid., p. 21.

4. The literal meaning of "inspired" is "God-breathed." The compound Greek word *theopneustos* means, literally, "God-breathed out." The point is that the resultant words are assured as those God desired because He breathed them. The inspiration is not of the human author as much as it is the inspiration of the resultant text itself.

5. Apostles were extraordinary in terms of revelation. To hold to

apostolic authority is still very important and was an important *emphasis* in the church up until the time of the Reformation. The Roman Church had added, over some time, the dogma of apostolic succession to the biblical doctrine of apostolic foundation. In reacting, properly, to apostolic succession Protestantism has often tended to ignore, to varying extents, the important truth of apostolic foundationalism.

6. Edward W. A. Koehler, *A Summary of Christian Doctrine* (St. Louis: Concordia: 1939), p. 10.

7. John R. W. Stott, *The Authority of the Bible* (Downers Grove, Ill.:: InterVarsity Press, 1974), p. 6–7.

8. Koehler, *Summary of Christian Doctrine,* p. 10.

9. James I. Packer, "The Reconstitution of Authority", in *Crux*, Vol. 18, no. 4 (December 1982) p. 2.

10. Ibid., p. 3.

11. Ibid., p. 3.

12. Stott, *Authority of the Bible,* p. 19.

13. Ibid, p. 20.

14. Martin Luther, *Luther's Works*, Vol. 21 (St. Louis:: Concordia) p. 61.

15. Stott, *Authority of the Bible,* p. 29.

16. Ibid., p. 30.

17. Francis Pieper, *Christian Dogmatics,* Vol. 1 (St. Louis:: Concordia, 1950) p. 307.

18. Heinrich Heppe, *Reformed Dogmatics* (Grand Rapids: Baker 1950,

rpt. 1978) p. 12.

19. *The Theses of Berne* (1528).

20. *The French Confession of Faith* (1559).

21. *The Belgic Confession* (1561).

22. *The Second Helvetic Confession* (1566).

23. *The Council of Trent*, "The Decree Concerning Canonical Scriptures."

24. Pieper, *Christian Dogmatics*, p. 308.

25. Ibid., quoted in Pieper, p. 315.

26. Pieper., *Christian Dogmatics*, p. 315.

27. Ibid., p. 315.

28. Ibid., p. 316.

29. Quoted in Ibid, p. 318.

30. Quoted in Ibid, p. 319.

31. Martin Luther, *The Bondage of the Will* (Westwood, N. J.: Revell, 1957) p. 71.

32. Martin Luther, *Luther's Works,* Vol. 5 (St. Louis.: Concordia) p. 335.

33. Pieper, *Christian Dogmatics*, p. 324.

34. Ibid., p. 324.

35. Ibid., p. 324.

36. Quoted in Victor Budgen, *Charismatics and the Word of God.* (Welwyn: Evangelical Press, 1985) p. 126.

37. John Blanchard (compiler), *Gathered Gold: A Treasury of Quotations for Christians* (Welwyn: Evangelical Press, 1984) p. 70.

38. Robert Schuller, *Self-Esteem: The New Reformation* (Waco, Tex.: Word) p. 30.

39. Quoted in Paul Cook, *The Whole Truth* (London: The British Evangelical Council, n.d.) p. 9.

40. Geoffrey W. Bromiley, "The Inspiration & Authority of Scripture" (n.d.) published in special reprint of *Eternity* and the *Holman Family Reference Bible* (Nashville, Tenn.: Holman, n.d.) p. 6.

5

The Sufficiency of the Written Word

Answering the Modern Roman Catholic Apologists

Dr. John F. MacArthur, Jr.

The tendency to venerate tradition is very strong in religion. The world is filled with religions that have been following set traditions for hundreds—even thousands—of years. Cultures come and go, but religious tradition shows an amazing continuity.

In fact, many ancient religions—including Druidism, Native American religions, and several of the oriental cults—eschewed written records of their faith, preferring to pass down their legends and rituals and dogmas via word of mouth. Such religions usually treat their body of traditions as a *de facto* authority equal to other religions' sacred writings.

Even among the world's religions that revere sacred writings, however, tradition and Scripture are often blended. This is true in Hinduism, for example, where the ancient Vedas are the Scriptures, and traditions handed down by gurus round out the faith of most followers.

Tradition in effect becomes a lens through which the written word is interpreted. Tradition therefore stands as the highest of all authorities, because it renders the only authoritative interpretation of the sacred writings.

This tendency to view tradition as supreme authority is not unique to pagan religions. Traditional Judaism, for example, follows the Scripture-plus-tradition paradigm. The familiar books of the Old Testament alone are viewed as Scripture, but true orthodoxy is actually defined by a collection of ancient rabbinical traditions known as the Talmud. In effect, the traditions of the Talmud carry an authority equal to or greater than that of the inspired Scriptures.

Teaching as Doctrines the Precepts of Men

This is no recent development within Judaism. The Jews of Jesus' day also placed tradition on an equal footing with Scripture. Rather, in effect, they made tradition superior to Scripture, because Scripture was interpreted by tradition and therefore made subject to it.

Whenever tradition is elevated to such a high level of authority, it inevitably becomes detrimental to the authority of Scripture. Jesus made this very point when he confronted the Jewish leaders. He showed that in many cases their traditions actually nullified Scripture. He therefore rebuked them in the harshest terms:

> "Rightly did Isaiah prophesy of you hypocrites, as it is written, 'This people honors Me with their lips, but their heart is far away from Me. But in vain do they worship Me, teaching as doctrines the precepts of men.'"
>
> "Neglecting the commandment of God, you hold to the tradition of men." He was also saying to them, "You nicely set aside the commandment of God in order to keep your tradition. For Moses said, 'Honor your father and your mother'; and, 'He who speaks evil of father or mother, let him be put to death'; but you say, 'If a man says to his father or his mother, anything of mine you might have been helped by is Corban (that is to say, given to God),' you no longer permit him to do anything for his father or his mother, thus invalidating the word of God by your tradition which you have handed down; and you do many things such as that (Mark 7:6–13).

It was inexcusable that tradition would be elevated to the level of Scripture in Judaism, because when God gave the law to Moses, it was in written form for a reason: to make it permanent and inviolable. The Lord made very plain that the truth He was revealing was not to be tampered with, augmented, or diminished in any way. His Word was the final authority in all matters: "You shall not add to the word which I am commanding you, nor take away from it, that you may keep the commandments of the Lord your God which I command you" (Deuteronomy 4:2). They were to observe His commandments assiduously, and neither supplement nor abrogate them by any other kind of "authority": "Whatever I command you, you shall be careful to do; you shall not add to nor take away from it" (Deuteronomy 12:32).

So the revealed Word of God, and nothing else, was the supreme and sole authority in Judaism. This alone was the standard of truth delivered to them by God Himself. Moses was instructed to write down the very words God gave him (Exodus 34:27), and that *written record* of God's Word became the basis for God's covenant with the nation (Exodus 24:4, 7). The written Word was placed in the Ark of the Covenant (Deuteronomy 31:9), symbolizing its supreme authority in the lives and the worship of the Jews forever. God even told Moses'successor, Joshua: "Be strong and very courageous; be careful to do according to all the law which Moses My servant commanded you; do not turn from it to the right or to the left, so that you may have success wherever you go. This book of the law shall not depart from your mouth, but you shall meditate on it day and night, so that you may be careful to do according to all that is written in it" (Joshua 1:7–8).

Of course, other books of inspired Scripture beside those written by Moses were later added to the Jewish canon—but this was a prerogative reserved by God alone. *Sola Scriptura* was therefore established in principle with the giving of the law. No tradition passed down by word of mouth, no rabbinical opinion, and no priestly innovation was to be accorded authority equal to the revealed Word of God as recorded in Scripture.

Agur understood this principle: "Every word of God is tested; He is a shield to those who take refuge in Him. Do not add to His words lest He reprove you, and you be proved a liar" (Proverbs 30:5–6).

The Scriptures therefore were to be the one standard by which everyone who claimed to

speak for God was tested: "To the law and to the
testimony: if they speak not according to this
word, it is because there is no light in them"
(Isaiah 8:20, KJV).

In short, tradition had no legitimate place of
authority in the worship of Jehovah. Everything
was to be tested by the Word of God as recorded
in the Scriptures. That's why Jesus' rebuke to
the scribes and Pharisees was so harsh. Their
very faith in Rabbinical tradition was in and of
itself a serious transgression of the covenant and
commandments of God (cf. Matthew 15:3).

The Rise and Ruin of Catholic Tradition

Unfortunately, Christianity has often followed
the same tragic road as paganism and Judaism
in its tendency to elevate tradition to a position
of authority equal to or greater than Scripture.
The Catholic Church in particular has its own
body of tradition that functions exactly like the
Jewish Talmud: it is the standard by which
Scripture is to be interpreted. In effect, tradition
supplants the voice of Scripture itself.

How did this happen? As James White has
demonstrated in his chapter on "*Sola Scriptura*
and the Early Church*," the earliest church
Fathers placed a strong emphasis on the author-

ity of Scripture over verbal tradition. Fierce debates raged in the early church over such crucial matters as the deity of Christ, His two natures, the Trinity, and the doctrine of original sin. Early church councils settled those questions by appealing to Scripture as the highest of all authorities. The councils themselves did not merely issue *ex cathedra* decrees, but they reasoned things out by Scripture and made their rulings accordingly. The authority was in the appeal to Scripture, not in the councils per se.

Unfortunately, the question of Scriptural authority itself was not always clearly delineated in the early church, and as the church grew in power and influence, church leaders began to assert an authority that had no basis in Scripture. The church as an institution became in many people's eyes the fountain of authority and the arbiter on all matters of truth. Appeals began to be made more often to tradition than to Scripture. As a result, extrabiblical doctrines were canonized and a body of opinion that found no support in Scripture began to be asserted as infallibly true.

Roman Catholic doctrine is shot through with legends and dogmas and superstitions that have no biblical basis whatsoever. The stations of the cross, the veneration of saints and angels, the Marian doctrines such as the Immaculate Conception, the Assumption, and the notion that Mary is co-mediatrix with Christ—none of those doctrines can be substantiated by Scripture. They are the product of Roman Catholic tradition.

Officially, the Catholic Church is very straightforward about her blending of Scripture and tradition. The recently published *Catechism of the Catholic Church* (henceforth CCC, citations referring to paragraph numbers rather than page numbers) acknowledges that the Roman Catholic Church "does not derive her certainty about all revealed truths from the holy Scriptures alone. *Both Scripture and Tradition must be accepted and honored with equal sentiments of devotion and reverence*" (CCC 82, emphasis added).

Tradition, according to Roman Catholicism, is therefore as much "the Word of God" as Scripture. According to the *Catechism,* Tradition and Scripture "are bound closely together and communicate one with the other. For both of them, flowing out from the same divine well-spring, come together in some fashion to form one thing and move towards the same goal" (CCC 80). The "sacred deposit of faith"—this admixture of Scripture and tradition—was supposedly entrusted by the apostles to their successors (CCC 84), and "The task of giving an authentic interpretation of the Word of God, whether in its written form or in the form of Tradition, has been entrusted to the living, teaching office of the Church alone. . . . This means that the task of interpretation has been entrusted to the bishops in communion with the successor of Peter, the Bishop of Rome" (CCC 85).

The *Catechism* is quick to deny that this makes the Church's teaching authority (called the *magisterium*) in any way superior to the Word of God itself (CCC 86). But it then goes on to warn the faithful that they must "read the Scripture within 'the living tradition of the whole Church' " (CCC 113). The *Catechism* at this point quotes "a saying of the Fathers[:] Sacred Scripture is written principally in the Church's heart rather than in documents and records, for the Church carries in her Tradition the living memorial of God's Word" (CCC 113).

So in effect, tradition is not only made equal to Scripture, but it becomes the *true* Scripture, written not in documents, but mystically within the Church herself. And when the Church speaks, her voice is heard as if it were the voice of God, giving the only true meaning to the

words of the "documents and records." Thus tradition utterly supplants and supersedes Scripture.

Modern Catholic Apologetics and Sola Scriptura

In other words, the official Catholic position
on Scripture is that Scripture does not and cannot speak for itself. It must be interpreted by the
Church's teaching authority and in light of
"living tradition." *De facto* this says that
Scripture has no inherent authority, but like all
spiritual truth, it derives its authority from the
Church. Only what the Church says is deemed
the *true* Word of God, the "Sacred Scripture . . .
written principally in the Church's heart rather
than in documents and records."

This position obviously emasculates Scripture. That is why the Catholic stance against
sola Scriptura has always posed a major problem
for Roman Catholic apologists. On one hand
faced with the task of defending Catholic doctrine, and on the other hand desiring to affirm
what Scripture says about itself, they find themselves on the horns of a dilemma. They cannot
affirm the authority of Scripture apart from the
caveat that tradition is necessary to explain the
Bible's true meaning. Quite plainly, that makes

tradition a superior authority. Moreover, in effect
it renders Scripture superfluous, for if Catholic
tradition inerrantly encompasses and explains
all the truth of Scripture, then the Bible is simply redundant. Understandably, *sola Scriptura*
has therefore always been a highly effective argument for defenders of the Reformation.

So it is not hard to understand why in recent
years Catholic apologists have attacked *sola
Scriptura* with a vengeance. If they can topple
this one doctrine, all the Reformers' other points
fall with it. For under the Catholic system, whatever the Church says must be the standard by
which to interpret all Scripture. Tradition is the
"true" Scripture, written in the heart of the
Church. The Church—not Scripture written in
"documents and records"—defines the truth
about justification by faith, veneration of saints,
transubstantiation, and a host of other issues
that divided the Reformers from Rome.

To put it another way, if we accept the voice
of the Church as infallibly correct, then what
Scripture says about these questions is ultimately irrelevant. And in practice this is precisely what happens. To cite but one example,
Scripture very plainly says, "There is one God,
and one mediator also between God and men,
the man Christ Jesus" (1 Timothy 2:5). Nonethe-

less, the Catholic Church insists that Mary is her Son's "co-mediatrix."[1]

And in the eyes of millions of Catholics, what the Church says is seen as the final and authoritative Word of God. First Timothy 2:5 is thus nullified by Church tradition.

Obviously, if Rome can prove her case against *sola Scriptura*, she overturns all the arguments for the Reformation in one fell swoop. If she can establish her tradition as an infallible authority, no mere biblical argument would have any effect against the dictates of the Church.

Modern Roman Catholic apologists have therefore mounted a carefully focused attack against *sola Scriptura*. Hoping to turn the Reformation's greatest strength into an argument against the Reformation, they have begun to argue that it is possible to debunk *sola Scriptura* by using Scripture alone! This line of argument is now being employed by Catholics against evangelicalism in practically every conceivable forum.

For example, these excerpts are from some articles posted on the Internet:

> The Protestant teaching that the Bible is the sole spiritual authority—*sola Scriptura*—is nowhere to be found in the Bible. St. Paul wrote to Timothy that Scripture is

"useful" (which is an understatement), but neither he nor anyone else in the early Church taught sola scriptura. And, in fact, nobody believed it until the Reformation.[2]

The Bible nowhere teaches that it is the sole authority in matters of belief. In fact, the Bible teaches that Tradition—the oral teachings given by Jesus to the apostles and their successors, the bishops—is a parallel source of authentic belief. [Quotations from 2 Thessalonians 2:15 and 1 Corinthians 11:2 follow].[3]

From some books written by Catholic apologists:

Nowhere does [the Bible] reduce God's Word down to Scripture alone. Instead, the Bible tells us in many places that God's authoritative Word is to be found in the church: her tradition (2 Thessalonians 2:15; 3:6) as well as her preaching and teaching (1 Peter 1:25; 2 Peter 1:20–21; Matthew 18:17).

That's why I think the Bible supports the Catholic principle of *sola verbum Dei*, "the Word of God alone" [with "Word of God" encompassing both tradition and Scripture], rather than the Protestant slogan, *sola scriptura*, "Scripture alone."[4]

The Bible actually denies that it is the complete rule of faith. John tells us that not everything concerning Christ's work is in Scripture (John 21:25), and Paul says that much Christian teaching is to be found in the tradition that is handed down by word of mouth (2 Timothy 2:2). He instructs us to "stand fast, and hold the traditions which you have learned, whether by word or by our epistle" (2 Thessalonians 2:15). We are told that the first Christians "were persevering in the doctrine of the apostles" (Acts 2:42), which was the oral teaching given long before the New Testament was written—and centuries before the canon of the New Testament was settled.[5]

And from a public debate on the question of *sola Scriptura*:

Sola Scriptura itself must be proved from Scripture alone. And if it can't be done, *sola scriptura* is a self-refuting proposition, and therefore it is false.[6]

[In] 2 Thessalonians 2:15, Paul commands the Church to stand firm and hold fast in the traditions that they had been given, whether orally, spoken, or through an epistle of theirs. So in other words, tradition is one major category, and there are two subsets in the one category: oral tradi-

tion, written tradition. That's what the
Word of God says.[7]

Many of these claims will be refuted elsewhere in this book. My main focus will be on
explaining the biblical passages cited in support
of the Catholic veneration of tradition. But allow
me a brief summary response to the thrust of all
these arguments.

The Sufficiency of Scripture

First, it is necessary to understand what *sola
Scriptura* does and does not assert. The Reformation principle of *sola Scriptura* has to do with
the *sufficiency* of Scripture as our supreme
authority in all spiritual matters. *Sola Scriptura*
simply means that *all truth necessary for our salvation and spiritual life is taught either explicitly or
implicitly in Scripture.*

It is not a claim that all truth of every kind is
found in Scripture. The most ardent defender of
sola Scriptura will concede, for example, that
Scripture has little or nothing to say about DNA
structures, microbiology, the rules of Chinese
grammar, or rocket science. This or that "scientific truth" for example, may or may not be
actually true, whether or not it can be supported
by Scripture—but Scripture is a "more sure

Word," standing above all other truth in its authority and certainty. It is "more sure," according to the apostle Peter, than the data we gather firsthand through our own senses (2 Peter 1:19). Therefore, Scripture is the highest and supreme authority on any matter to which it speaks.

But there are many important questions on which Scripture is silent. *Sola Scriptura* makes no claim to the contrary. Nor does *sola Scriptura* claim that everything Jesus or the apostles ever taught is preserved in Scripture. It only means that everything necessary, everything binding on our consciences, and everything God requires of us is given to us in Scripture.

Furthermore, we are forbidden to add to or take away from Scripture (cf. Deuteronomy 4:2; 12:32; Revelation 22:18–19). To do so is to lay on people's shoulders a burden that God Him-self does not intend for them to bear (cf. Matthew 23:4).

Scripture is therefore the perfect and only standard of spiritual truth, revealing infallibly all that we must believe in order to be saved, and all that we must do in order to glorify God. That—no more, no less—is what *sola Scriptura* means.

The *Westminster Confession of Faith* defines the sufficiency of Scripture in this way: "The whole counsel of God, concerning all things necessary for his own glory, man's salvation, faith, and life, is either expressly set down in scripture, or by good and necessary consequence may be deduced from scripture: unto which nothing at any time is to be added, whether by new revelations of the Spirit, or traditions of men" (1:6).

The Thirty-nine Articles of the Anglican Church include this statement on *sola Scriptura*: "Holy Scripture containeth all things necessary to salvation: so that whatsoever is not read therein, nor may be proved thereby, is not to be required of any man, that it should be believed as an article of the Faith, or be thought requisite or necessary to salvation" (article 6).

So *sola Scriptura* simply means that Scripture is *sufficient*. The fact that Jesus did and taught many things not recorded in Scripture (John 20:30; 21:25) is wholly irrelevant to the principle of *sola Scriptura*. The fact that most of the apostles' actual sermons in the early churches were not written down and preserved for us does not diminish the truth of biblical sufficiency one bit. What is certain is that all that is *necessary* is in Scripture—and we are forbidden "to exceed what is written" (1 Corinthians 4:6).

As other chapters in this volume have demonstrated and will demonstrate, Scripture

clearly claims for itself this sufficiency—and
nowhere more clearly than 2 Timothy 3:15–17. A
brief summary of that passage is perhaps
appropriate here as well. In short, verse 15
affirms that Scripture is sufficient for salvation:
"The sacred writings . . . are able to give you the
wisdom that leads to salvation through faith
which is in Christ Jesus." Verse 16 affirms the
absolute authority of Scripture, which is "God-
breathed" (Gk. *theopneustos*) and profitable for
our instruction. And verse 17 states that Scripture is able to equip the man of God "for every
good work." So the assertion that the Bible itself
does not teach *sola Scriptura* is simply wrong.

How Do We Know the Doctrine of the Apostles?

Now let's examine the key Scriptures Rome
cites to try to justify the existence of extrabiblical
tradition. Since many of these passages are similar, it will suffice to reply to the main ones. First
we'll examine the key verses that speak of how
apostolic doctrine was transmitted, and then
we'll explore what the apostle Paul meant when
he spoke of "tradition."

2 Timothy 2:2: "The things which you have
heard from me in the presence of many witnesses, these entrust to faithful men, who will be

able to teach others also." Here the apostle Paul instructs Timothy, a young pastor, to train other faithful men for the task of leadership in the church. There is no hint of apostolic succession in this verse, nor is there any suggestion that in training these men Timothy would be passing on to them an infallible tradition with authority equal to the Word of God.

On the contrary, what this verse describes is simply the process of discipleship. Far from imparting to these men some apostolic authority that would guarantee their infallibility, Timothy was to choose men who had proved themselves faithful, teach them the gospel, and equip them in the principles of church leadership he had learned from Paul. What Timothy was to entrust to them was the essential truth Paul himself had preached "in the presence of many witnesses."

What was this truth? It was not some undisclosed tradition, such as the Assumption of Mary, which would be either unheard of or disputed for centuries until a pope declared *ex cathedra* that it was truth. What Timothy was to hand on to other men was the same doctrine Paul had preached before "many witnesses." Paul was speaking of the gospel itself. It was the same message Paul commanded Timothy to preach, and it is the same message that is preserved in Scripture and sufficient to equip every man of God (2 Timothy 3:16–4:2).

In short, this verse is wholly irrelevant to the Catholic claim that tradition received from the apostles is preserved infallibly by her bishops. Nothing in this verse suggests that the truth Timothy would teach other faithful men would be preserved without error from generation to generation. That is indeed what Scripture says of itself: "All Scripture is inspired by God and profitable for teaching" (2 Timothy 3:16), but no such assertion is *ever* made for tradition handed down orally.

Like Timothy, we are to guard the truth that has been entrusted to us. But the only reliable canon, the only infallible doctrine, the only binding principles, and the only saving message, is the God-breathed truth of Scripture.

Acts 2:42: "They were continually devoting themselves to the apostles' teaching and to fellowship, to the breaking of bread and to prayer." This verse simply states that the early church followed the apostles' teaching as their rule of faith. Once again this passage says nothing about apostolic succession and contains no hint of a guarantee that "the apostles' teaching" would be infallibly preserved through any means other than Scripture.

Note also that this verse describes the attitude of the earliest *converts* to Christianity. The "they" at the beginning of the verse refers back to verse 41 and the three thousand souls who were converted at Pentecost. These were for the most part rank-and-file lay people. And their one source of Christian doctrine (this was before any of the New Testament had been penned) was the oral teaching of the apostles.

This verse is even more irrelevant to the question of infallible tradition than 2 Timothy 2:2. The only point it asserts that is remotely germane to the issue is that the source of authority for the early church was apostolic teaching. No one who holds to the doctrine of *sola Scriptura* would dispute that point. Let it be stated as clearly as possible: Protestants do not deny that the oral teaching of the apostles was authoritative, inerrant truth, binding as a rule of faith *on those who heard it*. Moreover, if there were any promise in Scripture that the *exact words* or *full sense* of the apostolic message would be infallibly preserved through word of mouth by an unbroken succession of bishops, we would be bound to obey that tradition as a rule of faith.

Scripture, however, which *is* God-breathed, never speaks of any other God-breathed authority; it never authorizes us to view tradition on an equal or superior plane of authority; and while it makes the claim of inerrancy for itself, it never acknowledges any other infallible source of authority. Word-of-mouth tradition is *never* said to be *theopneustos*, God-breathed, or infallible.

What Tradition Did Paul Command Adherence To?

We've already noted, however, that Catholic apologists claim they *do* see verses in Scripture that accord authority to tradition. Even non-Catholic versions of Scripture speak of a certain "tradition" that is to be received and obeyed with unquestioning reverence.

What of these verses? Protestants often find them difficult to explain, but in reality they make better arguments against the Catholic position than they do against *sola Scriptura*. Let's examine the main ones:

1 Corinthians 11:2: "Now I praise you because you remember me in everything, and hold firmly to the traditions, just as I delivered them to you." Those words of Paul to the Corinthians speak of tradition, do they not?

Yet as is often true, the meaning is plain when we look at the context. And examining the context, we discover this verse offers no support whatsoever for the Roman Catholic notion of infallible tradition.

First of all, the apostle is speaking not of traditions passed down to the Corinthians by someone else through word of mouth. This "tradition" is nothing other than doctrine the Corinthians had heard directly from Paul's own lips during his ministry in their church. The Greek word translated "traditions" is *paradosis*, translated "ordinances" in the King James Version. The Greek root contains the idea of transmission, and the idea is no doubt doctrine that was transmitted by oral means. In this case, however, it refers only to Paul's own preaching— not to someone else's report of what Paul taught.

The Corinthians had had the privilege of sitting under the apostle Paul's ministry for a year and a half (Acts 18:11), so it is ironic that of all the churches described in the New Testament, Corinth was one of the most problematic. Paul's first epistle to this church deals with a series of profound problems related to church discipline and practice, including serious sin in their midst, disunity among the brethren, disorder in church meetings, Christians who were taking one another to court, abuse of spiritual gifts, and so on. Second Corinthians is an extended defense of Paul's ministry in the face of opposition

and hostility. Someone in the church—possibly
even someone whom Paul had entrusted with a
position of leadership—had evidently fomented
a rebellion against Paul during his long absence.

The Corinthians knew Paul. He had been
their pastor. Yet they were obviously slipping
away from the moorings he had so carefully established during his pastorate there. Far from
being instruments through which Paul's tradition was infallibly preserved and handed down,
the Corinthians were rebelling against his apos-
tleship! That is why Paul encouraged them to
remember what he had heard from them and
follow it to the letter. What did he teach during
that year and a half in their midst? We have no
way of knowing precisely, but we have every reason to believe that the substance of his teaching
was the same truth that is recorded throughout
his epistles and elsewhere in the New Testament. Once again, we do know for certain that
everything essential for thoroughly equipping
Christians for life and godliness was preserved
in Scripture (2 Timothy 3:15–17). The rest is not
recorded for us, and nothing anywhere in Scripture indicates that it was handed down through
oral tradition—especially not through any
means that guaranteed it would be inspired and
infallible.

1 Corinthians 11:2 in particular teaches no such thing. It is nothing but Paul's exhortation to the Corinthians that they remember and obey his apostolic teaching. It reflects Paul's own personal struggle to protect and preserve the doctrinal tradition he had carefully established in Corinth. But again, there is no implication whatsoever that Paul expected this tradition to be infallibly preserved through any inspired means other than Scripture. On the contrary, Paul was concerned lest his ministry among the Corinthians prove to have been in vain (cf. 2 Corinthians 6:1).

2 Thessalonians 2:15: "So then, brethren, stand firm and hold to the traditions which you were taught, whether by word of mouth or by letter from us." This is perhaps the favorite verse of Catholic apologists when they want to support the Catholic appeal to tradition, because the verse plainly delineates between the written word and oral "traditions."

Again the Greek word is *paradosis.* Clearly, the apostle is speaking of doctrine, and it is not to be disputed that the doctrine he has in mind is authoritative, inspired truth.

So what is this inspired tradition that they received "by word of mouth"? Doesn't this verse rather clearly support the Catholic position?

No, it does not. Again, the context is essential to a clear understanding of what Paul was saying. The Thessalonians had evidently been misled by a forged letter, supposedly from the apostle Paul, telling them that the day of the Lord had already come (2 Thessalonians 2:2).

The entire church had apparently been upset by this, and the apostle Paul was eager to encourage them. For one thing, he wanted to warn them not to be taken in by phony "inspired truth." And so he told them clearly how to recognize a genuine epistle from him—it would be signed in his own handwriting: "I, Paul, write this greeting with my own hand, and this is a distinguishing mark in every letter; this is the way I write" (3:17). He wanted to ensure that they would not be fooled again by forged epistles.

But even more important, he wanted them to stand fast in the teaching they had already received from him. He had already told them, for example, that the day of the Lord would be preceded by a falling away, and the unveiling of the man of lawlessness. "Do you not remember that while I was still with you, I was telling you these things?" (2:5). There was no excuse for them to be troubled by a phony letter, for they had heard the actual truth from his own mouth already.

Now, no one—even the most impassioned champion of *sola Scriptura*—would deny that Paul had taught the Thessalonians many things by word of mouth. No one would deny that the teaching of an apostle carried absolute authority. The point of debate between Catholics and Protestants is whether that teaching was infallibly preserved by word of mouth. So the mere reference to truth received firsthand from Paul himself is, again, irrelevant as support for the Catholic position.

Certainly nothing here suggests that the tradition Paul delivered to the Thessalonians is infallibly preserved for us anywhere except in Scripture itself. In fact, the real thrust of what Paul is writing here is antithetical to the spirit of Roman Catholic tradition. Paul is not encouraging the Thessalonians to receive some tradition that had been delivered to them via second or third hand reports. On the contrary, *he was ordering them to receive as infallible truth only what they had heard directly from his own lips.*

Paul was very concerned to correct the Thessalonians' tendency to be led astray by false epistles and spurious tradition. From the very beginning the Thessalonians had not responded to the gospel message as nobly as the Bereans, who "received the word with great eagerness, examining the Scriptures daily, to see whether these things were so" (Acts 17:11).

It is highly significant that the Bereans are explicitly *commended* for examining the apostolic message in light of Scripture. They had the priority right: Scripture is the supreme rule of faith, by which everything else is to be tested. Unsure of whether they could trust the apostolic message—which, by the way, was as inspired and infallible and true as Scripture itself—the Bereans erased all their doubt by double-checking the message against Scripture. Yet Roman Catholics are forbidden by their Church to take such an approach! They are told that the Church through her bishops dispenses the only true and infallible understanding of Scripture.

Therefore it is pointless to test the Catholic Church's message by Scripture; for if there appears to be a conflict—and make no mistake, there are many—Rome says her traditions carry more weight than her critics' interpretation of Scripture.

What the Apostle was telling the Thessalonians was nothing like what Rome tells faithful Catholics. Paul was urging the Thessalonians to test all truth-claims by Scripture, and by the words they had heard personally from his own lips. And since the only words of the apostles that are infallibly preserved for us are found in Scripture, that means that we, like the Bereans, must compare everything with Scripture to see whether it is so.

Roman Catholic apologists protest that only a fraction of Paul's messages to the Thessalonians are preserved in the two brief epistles Paul wrote to that church. True, but may not we assume that what he taught the Thessalonians was the very truths that are found in generous measure throughout all his epistles—justification by faith alone, the true gospel of grace, the sovereignty of God, the Lordship of Christ, and a host of other truths? The New Testament gives us a full-orbed Christian theology. Who can prove that anything essential is omitted? On the contrary, we are assured that Scripture is sufficient for salvation and spiritual life (2 Timothy 3:15–17). Where does Scripture ever suggest that there are unwritten truths that are necessary for our spiritual well-being? One thing is certain—the words in 2 Thessalonians 2:15 imply no such thing.

2 Thessalonians 3:6: "Now we command you, brethren, in the name of our Lord Jesus Christ, that you keep aloof from every brother who leads an unruly life and not according to the tradition

which you received from us." This is the only
other verse in all the New Testament where Paul
uses the words *tradition* or *traditions* to speak of
apostolic truth that is to be obeyed.

By now, Paul's use of this term should be
well established. This *cannot* be a reference to
truth passed down from generation to generation. Again, Paul is speaking of a "tradition" received firsthand from him.

This is the closing section of the epistle. Paul
is summing up. And he once again underscores
the importance of the teaching the Thessalonians had received directly from his mouth. The
"tradition" he speaks of here is doctrine so
crucial that anyone who refuses to heed it and
live by it should be rejected from the fellowship.

What is this "tradition"? Is it Marian theology, or dogma about the efficacy of relics, or
other teachings unique to Roman Catholicism?
Not at all—it is simple, practical apostolic doctrine, taught and lived out by example while
Paul was among the Thessalonians. Paul goes
on to define specifically what "tradition" he has
in mind:

> We did not act in an undisciplined manner
> among you, nor did we eat anyone's bread
> without paying for it, but with labor and
> hardship we kept working night and day so

that we might not be a burden to any of
you; not because we do not have the right
to this, but in order to offer ourselves as a
model for you, that you might follow our
example. For even when we were with you,
we used to give you this order: if anyone
will not work, neither let him eat. For we
hear that some among you are leading an
undisciplined life, doing no work at all, but
acting like busybodies. Now such persons
we command and exhort in the Lord Jesus
Christ to work in quiet fashion and eat
their own bread. But as for you, brethren,
do not grow weary of doing good (3:7–13).

In other words, Paul was speaking of simple,
practical doctrine about stewardship of one's
time, a man's responsibility to work and provide
for his family, and personal discipline in daily
life. These truths are now part of holy Scripture,
by virtue of Paul's including them in this epistle.
Put that together with everything else the New
Testament records, and you have every part of
the apostolic message that was infallibly preserved for us.

Is the sum of Scriptural truth a sufficient rule
of faith for the Christian? We have the Bible's
own assurance that it is. Scripture alone is sufficient to lead us to salvation and fully equip us
for life and eternity (2 Timothy 3:15–17).

Therefore we may know with certainty that every *essential* aspect of the apostolic message is included in Scripture.

Note that Paul clearly regarded his epistles as inspired, authoritative Scripture. He charged the Thessalonians with these instructions: "And if anyone does not obey our instruction in this letter, take special note of that man and do not associate with him, so that he may be put to shame" (2 Thessalonians 3:14).

So the written words of Scripture are binding. Apostolic preaching was equally binding *for those who heard it from the apostles' own mouths.* Beyond that, Scripture lays no burden on anyone's shoulders. But, thank God, His own Word assures us that Scripture is fully sufficient to bring us to salvation and to equip us spiritually for all that God demands of us.

No man, no church, no religious authority has any warrant from God to augment the inspired Word of Scripture with additional traditions, or to alter the plain sense of it by subjecting it to the rigors of a "traditional" meaning not found in the Word itself. To do so is clearly to invalidate the Word of God—and we know what our Lord thinks of that (Matthew 15:6–9).

[1] From the Vatican II documents, *Lumen Gentium*, 62.

[2] From an article by George Sim Johnston posted on the Catholic Information Network.

[3] From a tract issued by Catholic Answers.

[4] Scott Hahn, *Rome Sweet Home* (San Francisco: Ignatius, 1993) p. 74.

[5] Karl Keating, *Catholicism and Fundamentalism* (San Francisco: Ignatius, 1988) p. 136.

[6] Patrick Madrid, in a debate with James White. Information on ordering this tape can be had by writing Alpha and Omega Ministries, P.O. Box 37106, Phoenix, AZ 85069.

[7] Ibid.

6

Scripture and Tradition
The Bible and Tradition in Roman Catholicism

Dr. Sinclair Ferguson

The year 1996 marks the four hundred and fiftieth anniversary of the death of Martin Luther, whose famous Ninety-Five Theses sparked off a religious fire in Europe which the Roman Catholic Church was unable to extinguish. The theological conflict which ensued has often been characterized as focusing on the so-called fourfold "alones" of the Reformation: *sola gratia, solo Christo, sola fide, sola Scriptura*—salvation is by grace alone, in Christ alone, by faith alone, and all that is necessary for salvation is taught in Scripture alone. Each of these principles, and certainly all four together, served as a canon by which the teaching of the Roman Catholic Church was assessed and found to be wanting.

In these great slogans the nouns—grace, Christ, faith, Scripture—were and are of great importance. But in each case the qualifying *sola* (alone) was in some ways even more significant. For Rome had always taught that salvation was by grace through faith in Christ, and had always held that the Bible was the Word of God—but never *alone*. To speak of *sola Scriptura* has almost always been viewed in Rome as a prescription for spiritual anarchy in which everyone would create for himself the message of the Bible. The only safeguard against this was the living tradition of the Church viewed as a further channel of the divine revelation.

The printing press (and therefore widespread access to the Bible) is a Renaissance phenomenon, and literacy levels were low in the Middle Ages. But this alone does not account for the Reformation horror stories about the large-scale ignorance of the Bible among both priest and people. Nevertheless it would be uncharitable to extrapolate from those dark days to the present day as though no counter-reformations had taken place in the interim. And it would reveal considerable ignorance on the part of Protestants if they did not recognize that in the past century a widespread interest in the Bible has developed within the Roman Catholic Church.

Can it be, then, that we now face a new situation in Roman Catholicism? For the first time

since the Reformation "common" Bibles are being published. Moreover, not only within the
World Council of Churches (largely dominated
by liberal theology), but also within evangelicalism substantial rapprochement has been viewed
as possible in our own time. So it is timely to
ask: Has something unprecedented happened
within Roman Catholicism's interpretation of
the Bible so that the old differences can, at last,
be laid to rest?

During the past century and a quarter—
from the First Vatican Council (1870) to the
publication of the Pontifical Biblical Commission's important work *The Interpretation of the
Bible in the Church* (1993)—the Roman Magisterium has published a series of significant
statements on the nature, interpretation and role
of the Bible in the Church. These began in the
nineteenth century in the widespread crisis for
faith created by the effect of Enlightenment
thought and thereafter by the onslaught of
scientific humanism which found its impetus in
the evolutionism of the late nineteenth century.
Pronouncements have continued to appear up to
the present day, when the Vatican has sought to
wed together contemporary historical-critical
methods of biblical interpretation with the
ancient dogmas of the Church. Each of these

statements is of interest on its own account; together they mark a development which has been
significant for the work of large numbers of
Roman Catholic biblical scholars.

The story of this development is not well
known among Protestants. Indeed probably
most Roman Catholics are relatively unfamiliar
with it. It is worth narrating, at least in broad
outline.

Developments in Rome

In 1893 Pope Leo XIII issued the Encyclical
Letter *Providentissimus Deus*. It was the first wide-
ranging attempt of the Roman Church to deal
specifically with the impact of the critical
methodologies which had come to characterize
theological scholarship in the latter part of the
nineteenth century. In them the Bible was
treated as an ancient Near Eastern text and assessed from the standpoint of critical historical
investigation and linguistic and religious development. In sophisticated theological terms,
Scripture's "humanity" was explored (and, in
fact, its divinity was increasingly ignored and
denied).

Against this background, in which the idea
of human evolution played a major role, *Provi-*

dentissimus Deus insisted on a long-standing principle of Christian orthodoxy: If God is Author of both Nature and Scripture, these two "books" of divine revelation must be in harmony with each other. The encyclical emphasized that there could therefore be no ultimate conflict between the Bible and either the natural sciences or historical investigation. It urged both theologians and scientists to respect the limits of their own spheres. In addition, biblical exegetes who employed the fruits of secular scientific and historical studies were counseled to remember the importance of the *analogia fidei* (analogy of faith): the Scriptures should always be interpreted in keeping with the apostolic rule of faith to which the church subscribed. The last word on what the Bible taught lay with the Roman Magisterium.

Providentissimus Deus was thus characterized by a conservative (some would have said "reactionary") character, expressed particularly in its negative criticisms of the way in which historical-critical principles were being used. The underlying anxiety of the entire encyclical was that the results of this critical movement would prove to be injurious to the faith of which the Church was called to be the guardian, not the destroyer.

Fifty years later the face of Europe had changed dramatically. The Great War had been fought from 1914–18; the Second World War of 1939–45 was in full course. The misplaced and anthropocentric optimism of nineteenth-century liberal theology had collapsed, shattered before the enormity of human need; the notion that humanity was evolving from a lower to a higher moral condition had been dealt an embarrassing blow. The "gospel" of the universal Fatherhood of God and the brotherhood of man stood exposed in all of its inherent poverty. There arose a new sense of need for some powerful word from God. In Protestantism the "theology of crisis" emerged and what came to be known as the "Biblical Theology" movement was stirring into life.

Significant developments had also taken place within the world of Roman Catholic biblical scholarship. The Pontifical Biblical Commission was created by Leo XIII in 1902. In the wake of *Providentissimus Deus*, its earliest responses (*responsa*) to questions of biblical interpretation were characterized by negative reaction to higher criticism. But in due season (it was completely reorganized in 1971 following the Second Vatican Council) it would prove to be a spearhead of the new way of reading the

Bible.

In 1943, Pius XII issued his Encyclical Letter *Divino Afflante Spiritu*. It was promulgated when the Second World War was in full flood, but not until the turn of the decade did its full impact begin to be felt. Now a more positive note was struck. For one thing, Roman Catholic biblical scholars were largely set free from the burden which the Church had carried for centuries: the use of the Vulgate (Jerome's Latin translation of the Bible). It had been regarded as the authoritative text for ecclesiastical use since the time of the Council of Trent (even now it was still declared to be "free from all error in matters of faith and morals").

In a manner reminiscent of the humanists of the Renaissance, with the motto *ad fontes* ("back to the original sources"), Roman Catholic scholars now enjoyed a new freedom and fresh impetus to gain and employ expertise in the biblical languages to enable a true understanding of the text of Scripture. A new value was recognized in the use of such tools as textual, literary and form criticism. The importance of history, ethnology, archaeology "and other sciences" was affirmed. The "true meaning," indeed the so-called "literal sense" of Scripture was to be sought as well as the "spiritual significance."

Precritical ways of reading the Bible were widely (but not entirely) replaced by the new approach. Now a clear distinction was made between the "meaning" of the original text and the contemporary application ("significance") of it. Principles of interpretation which had long been familiar to Protestants were now increasingly recognized as essential to proper biblical exegesis. The historical-critical method had come to stay.

All this was encouraged (it could scarcely have been prevented, but the genius of Rome, unlike Wittenberg and Geneva, has always been its ability to hold opposite tendencies together). The underlying principle was that the Scriptures cannot be charged with error. Supposed errors in Scripture, it was held, could be resolved by a right reading of the text. Any tensions between Scripture and "reality" could always be resolved in favor of biblical integrity. Harmonization was an essential key to reading the Bible as a modern Catholic.

Times change, and we change with them. The second half of the twentieth century has seen continued movement in Roman Catholic biblical scholarship. This has not been without ecclesiastical bloodletting (at one point professors at the Biblical Institute were banned from teaching!). But the overall result has been that some of the most erudite biblical studies published during this period carry the *imprimatur* and *nihil obstat* which identify them as the work of Roman Catholic scholars which has been declared "free of doctrinal or moral error."

The most recent succinct expression of this development can be seen in the Pontifical Biblical Commission's statement on biblical interpretation, published in 1993. Here the fruits of critical scholarship set within the context of the Church's tradition are warmly welcomed. Indeed, strikingly—in view of the importance of the principle of harmonization at all costs which marked earlier Roman Catholic pronouncements—it is now of a Protestant-style fundamentalist approach to Scripture that the Church seems to have become most critical, and perhaps most fearful.

But why should this development since 1870 be of interest to Protestant Christians? For a reason which lies on the surface of much of the very best Catholic biblical scholarship. There is a clear recognition in Roman Catholic biblical scholarship that there is a gulf—or at least a distance—between what the text of Sacred Scripture states and the teaching of the Sacred Tradition of the Church. There is also recognition that the words of Jesus recorded in John

16:12–15, often taken as a specific promise guaranteeing the truth and infallibility of Sacred Tradition, do not refer to such Tradition at all.[1] By necessity, therefore, some Roman Catholic in terpreters of Scripture have found it necessary to develop a novel view of the relationship between Scripture and Tradition in order to hold them together: Tradition adds to Scripture, but Scripture is "open" to Tradition.

Can this contention be readily illustrated from Roman Catholic biblical scholarship?

In critical discussion it is always a great temptation to treat the most extreme examples of the opposition's viewpoint as though they were representative. That is an unworthy tactic and often merely hardens prejudices on both sides. In this context, however, the point can readily be illustrated not from the worst historical examples of Roman Catholic biblical interpretation, but—albeit from a necessarily limited sample—by what is widely regarded as its best.

It would be hard to find a better illustration of the new approach to the Bible in Roman Catholicism than the recent widely acclaimed commentary on Romans by Joseph A. Fitzmyer. Professor Fitzmyer is a leading Roman Catholic scholar whose outstanding academic gifts pervade his almost 800-page commentary. While it is often true in the matter of commentaries that "one man's meat is another man's poison," it is impossible to imagine any student of Scripture failing to find considerable profit from the erudition and stimulus of Fitzmyer's work. Raymond E. Brown, the outstanding American Catholic Johannine scholar, describes Fitzmyer as "the most learned N[ew] T[estament] scholar on the American Catholic scene."[2] Elsewhere he says of his work on Romans that "It can lay fair claim to being the best commentary on Romans in English."[3] Even those who might award the palm to someone other than Fitzmyer recognize the value of the commendation.

But it is precisely *because* of the quality of this commentary that its contents are so significant. A desire for careful exegesis coupled with faithfulness to the Magisterium of the Church leads Fitzmyer (a Jesuit) to state, albeit with appropriate sensitivity and discretion, that the teaching of the Scriptures cannot *simpliciter* be identified with the teachings of the Sacred Tradition. The following selection of illustrations will underline this.

A Roman Catholic on Romans

In an extensive introductory chapter on

Pauline theology, Fitzmyer includes an essay on faith. In the developed theology of the medieval period, theologians had spoken and written much of *fides caritate formata*, justifying faith which was "faith formed by love." This, not "faith alone," justifies. This view was confirmed at the Council of Trent.

Many of the Tridentine statements reveal misunderstandings of the teaching of Luther and the other Reformers; nevertheless, its teaching in this connection is clearly intended as a rejection of the principles the Reformers regarded as central to the gospel. Trent's Decree on Justification reads as follows:

> If anyone says that people are justified either by the sole imputation of the righteousness (*justitia*) of Christ or by the sole remission of sins, to the exclusion of the grace and charity which is poured into their hearts through the Holy Spirit and inheres in them; or even that the grace by which we are justified is only the favour of God, let him be anathema.[4]

Rome's great fear has always been that *sola fide* would breed antinomianism and moral license. Christians, it was held, were preserved from this by the fact that justification takes place through faith which is formed by love; i.e., justification involves personal transformation.

But, comments Fitzmyer, Paul's notion of faith which "blossoms" in love is to be distinguished from this *fides caritate formata*:

> That is a philosophical transposition of the Pauline teaching—acceptable or not depending on whether one agrees with the philosophy involved—but the genuine Pauline idea of "faith working itself out through love" is implicit in Romans . . . he does not equate faith with love; nor does he ascribe to love what he does to faith (viz., justification, salvation), even though he recognizes the necessity of the two working in tandem.[5]

Here is an important recognition of the fact that we must distinguish between what the Tradition has said and what the Scriptures actually affirm. The idea of faith and love being instrumental in justification cannot be read out of the text as such. It is no part of the exegesis of Paul's words.

Note however that Fitzmyer is careful to suggest only that there is distance between what is affirmed by Paul and what is stated in the Tradition. He does not affirm that there is any necessary contradiction between Scripture and Tradition.

More is to follow. Commenting on the central passage, Romans 3:21–26, Fitzmyer states that Paul here formulates "three, or possibly four, effects of the Christ-event [i.e., the work of Christ]. . . : justification, redemption, expiation, and possibly pardon" and adds, "It is important to recognize that such effects of the Christ-event are appropriated through faith in Christ Jesus, and only through faith. It is the means whereby human beings experience what Christ has done."[6]

Here again the Pauline text is to be read on its own terms without recourse to post-Pauline developments in the Church. Fitzmyer knows that within the Church there have always been those who have read Paul's words as implying the principle of *sola fide*.

It would be quite wrong, however (indeed naïve), to read this distancing of the Church's pronouncements from the statements of the biblical text as a capitulation to the Protestant exposition. For Fitzmyer is no less careful to point out the difference between the text and the way in which it has been interpreted within the Protestant churches.

Within a page of the previous citation we find Professor Fitzmyer rejecting the interpretation of a Protestant scholar on the grounds that

"that reading would introduce an Anselmian distinction into the Pauline text, which does not warrant it."[7] But even here the concern is to allow Paul to speak for himself in distinction from reading him through the eyes of the construction of a postbiblical tradition (in this case one which also appealed to Protestantism). Whether or not Fitzmyer's critique is accurate, what is at first sight remarkable is the way in which his recognition of Paul's emphasis on the unique role of faith might easily be mistaken for the comment of a Protestant exegete.

There are other noteworthy illustrations of an exegesis which self-consciously seeks to let the Scriptures speak for themselves apart from the dominance of theological tradition. In this sense the Roman Catholic scholar is approaching the text in a manner similar to the Protestant.

Commenting on the words "justified freely by his grace" in Romans 3:24, Fitzmyer notes:

> It should be superfluous to stress . . . that in using *dorean* and *te autou chariti*, Paul is not referring to the efficient cause of justification by the former and the formal cause by the latter (as if *charis* were "sanctifying grace"). That is anachronistic exegesis, a distinction born of later medieval and Tridentine theology.[8]

Here again, without rejecting Tridentine teaching as such, a distinction is made between what the text itself states and the theology which has developed within the Catholic tradition.

The comments which may strike the Protestant mind as most unexpected are to be found in Professor Fitzmyer's exposition of Romans 3:27–31. It was in his translation of Romans 3:28 in 1522 that Luther's appeal to *sola fide* emerged as seminal for the Reformation understanding of the gospel. Fitzmyer recognizes that in fact this language long predates Luther and can be found already in the writings of the early Fathers. He frankly states that "in this context" Paul means "by faith alone" although he contends that in the Lutheran sense its use is an extension of what Paul says. This inevitably prompts questions as to what the nature of this "extension" is, and whether there is any Roman Catholic "sense" in which justification is genuinely "by faith alone." But the admission in and of itself is significant.

The same distance between Scripture and Tradition is further indicated when Fitzmyer turns to the exposition of Romans 5:12. The traditional Roman Catholic view of this text is to see here a reference to "original" sin. This was made explicit by the Council of Trent, which not only set its imprimatur to this exegesis of Paul's words, but also forbade any other understanding of his statement. Fitzmyer comments:

> This tradition found its formal conciliar expression in the Tridentine *Decretum de peccato originali*, Sess. V, 2–4 . . . This decree gave a definitive interpretation to the Pauline text in the sense that his words teach a form of the dogma of Original Sin, a rare text that enjoys such an interpretation.
>
> Care must be taken, however, to understand what Paul is saying and not to transform his mode of expression too facilely into the precision of later dogmatic development . . . Paul's teaching is regarded as seminal and open to later dogmatic development, but it does not say all that the Tridentine decree says.[9]

Again we can hardly avoid noting the caution which emerges with respect to reading Church Tradition back into Scripture. The dogma as such is not rejected; what is made clear is that it is not to be identified *simpliciter* with the teaching contained in the New Testament.

Next, in commenting on Romans 6:12, Fitzmyer alludes to the teaching of the Council of Trent that what Paul sometimes calls "sin" (as, for example, in Romans 6:12) is not described as such by the Roman Catholic Church, but rather is understood as the *fomes peccati*. The allusion here is to one of the most astonishing (and surely embarrassing) statements in the documents of Trent, in the Decree Concerning Original Sin:

> This concupiscence, which the apostle sometimes calls sin, the holy Synod declares that the Catholic Church has never understood it to be called sin, as being truly and properly sin in those born again, but because it is of sin, and inclines to sin. And if anyone is of a contrary sentiment, let him be anathema.[10]

Again we must not make the mistake of thinking that Fitzmyer has ceased to be a faithful son of the Church. For this, he notes (in agreement with the earlier biblical scholar M-J. Lagrange), "might be an exact theological transposition," but it is a precision not yet found in the Pauline text.

Our concern here is not to discuss the precision of the theology involved in this statement, but once more to underline the gap—although for Fitzmyer manifestly not an unbridgeable historical gulf—which is fixed between the revelation as it comes to us in Scripture and what the Church has received as its authoritative Tradition.

No doubt this whole approach strikes anxiety in the hearts of Roman Catholics who are conservative and traditionalist (there are "fundamentalists" in both Roman Catholicism and Protestantism). They may find some relief in the way Professor Fitzmyer's concurrence with the Roman Tradition is given notable expression in his handling of Paul's teaching on justification. Professor Fitzmyer nuances the meaning of *dikaioo* in the direction of "being made upright." Here, at perhaps the most critical point, his exegesis harmonizes with the Vulgate's translation of the New Testament's *dikaioo* by *justum facere*.

Despite the presence of Lutheran sympathizers at Trent, the Council committed the Church irrevocably to a transformationist doctrine of justification:

> Justification . . . is not the removal of our sins alone, but also the sanctification and renovation of the inner man through the willing reception of the grace and the other gifts by which a man from being unjust (*ex injusto*) becomes just, and from being an enemy becomes a friend so that he may be an heir according to the hope of eternal life.[11]

Even Fitzmyer's further qualification—he notes that this justification takes place "gratuitously through God's powerful declaration of acquittal"—does not eliminate a distinctively Tridentine exegesis, as he makes clear:

> The sinful human being is not only "declared upright," but is "made upright" (as in 5:19), for the sinner's condition has changed.[12]

Much is at stake here. In many areas where Sacred Tradition is not already present and perspicuous in Sacred Scripture, Fitzmyer and other Roman Catholic scholars reduce the gap between what is taught in the biblical text and the dogma of Sacred Tradition by an appeal to the "open" character of biblical teaching. In this way they minimize the force of the Reformation criticism that Tradition contradicts Scripture.

Jesus' washing of the disciples' feet and His exhortation to them to imitate Him (John 13:1–15) give an example of this "open" character of Scripture. Foot washing might well have developed into a Sacrament, in a manner parallel to the development which took place in another "open" passage, James 5:14. Here, "under the Spirit-guided development of Tradition" the text became the basis for the Sacrament of the

Anointing of the Sick.[13]

No appeal to the theory of Scripture's "open" character can be of service, however, in relationship to the doctrine of justification. It would simply not be possible for Fitzmyer at this juncture to agree with the Reformation exegesis of justification as declaratory, imputed righteousness yet appeal to the "open" character of Paul's teaching and to the Spirit's continuing work in the Church as bringing out the fullness of meaning in justification as including infused righteousness. For these two things stand in contradiction.

Fitzmyer's interpretation is, nevertheless, based on an exegetical appeal—to his own exegesis of Romans 5:19: "Just as through the disobedience of one man many were made sinners, so through the obedience of one many will be made upright."[14] He takes Paul's verb *kathistanai* ("made") in the sense of subjective condition, i.e., in a transformationist sense.

Two things should be said here. First, we believe Fitzmyer's interpretation of Romans 5:19 can be demonstrated to be mistaken.[15] But second, his logic is wrong. Even were *kathistanai* understood in a subjective-transformationist sense, it does not necessarily follow that Paul's use of *dikaioo* is transformationist rather than forensic and declaratory. Consistently to interpret "justify" in the light of this assumption is an exegetical procedure without justification!

But even here there is a formal recognition of the principle: Sacred Scripture must be distinguished from Sacred Tradition; we should not assume that the latter is an exegesis of the former.

Naturally Protestants view this distinction through Protestantized spectacles. Anyone convinced of the sole authority and sufficiency of Scripture is bound to ask how it is possible for a scholar of integrity to recognize this gap and yet to remain a faithful Roman Catholic.

It is too simple a construction, however, to conclude that there is manifest duplicity here. Rather, the general consistency and clarity with which Fitzmyer's exegesis illustrates the gap between Scripture and Tradition highlights why it is that the Protestant appeal to Scripture alone to refute Roman Catholic dogma seems to cut little ice: For Rome, neither Scripture nor Tradition can stand on its own. The rationale for this should now be clear: In the Roman Catholic Church, Sacred Tradition stands beside Sacred Scripture as a valid and authoritative source of divine revelation. In fact both emerge within one and the same context: the Catholic Church.

Understanding this principle helps us to see the mindset of the Roman Catholic Church's approach to interpreting the Bible at this juncture.

Scripture and Tradition

For Rome, the Bible itself emerges from within the Church. The Church exists prior to the Bible; the Bible is itself an expression of the living voice of the Church—in its own way it is Tradition. In the words of the recent *Catechism of the Catholic Church*, "the New Testament itself demonstrates the process of living Tradition."[16] The New Testament is Tradition—the earliest tradition inscripturated in distinction from the living Tradition which arises within the ongoing life of the Church in the context of apostolic succession.

This perspective is well attested in the succession of Rome's authoritative doctrinal statements.

Appeal in this context is made to the Profession of Faith composed in connection with the Second Council of Constantinople (553), to the Council of Lateran (649) and to the Second Council of Nicea (787). It was, however, in the context of the Counter-Reformation that the

Church's position was set in concrete by the Council of Trent:

> The holy ecumenical and general Council of Trent . . . clearly perceives that this truth and rule are contained in the written books and unwritten traditions which have come down to us. . . . Following, then, the example of the orthodox Fathers, it receives and venerates with the same sense of loyalty and reverence all the books of the Old and New Testaments—for God alone is the author of both—together with all the traditions concerning faith and morals, as coming from the mouth of Christ or being inspired by the Holy Spirit and preserved in continuous succession in the Catholic Church.[17]

The implication of this, specifically drawn out by the Council itself, was that no one should dare to interpret the Scripture in a way contrary to the unanimous consent of the Fathers, even though such interpretations are not intended for publication.

Leaving to one side the doubtful concept of "the unanimous consent of the Fathers," it is clear here why the Tradition becomes the master element in the Scripture-Tradition liaison. Historically it has always been the case that a "living" (in the sense of contemporaneous) word of revelation will become the rule for Christians *de facto* (whatever may be claimed to the contrary). That is virtually a psychological inevitability. In the case of Rome, what may have begun as a limiting concept (the *regulum fidei*) developed into the master concept.

This position, with appeal to these very citations, was later confirmed by the Church at the First Vatican Council in the Dogmatic Constitution *Dei Filius* (1870). A quarter of a century later, *Providentissimus Deus* (1893) appealed to the principle of the analogy of faith understood as the *consensus fidelium* as an essential principle for Catholic exposition. Roman Catholic exegetes were summoned to use critical skills with the specific agenda of confirming the received interpretation.

All this was stated within the context of Leo XIII's affirmation of the inerrancy and infallibility of Scripture. Such was the continuing impact of modernism, however, that within two decades the *Decree Lamentabili* (1907) was issued to stem the tide of theological corruption. It repudiated and condemned the view that "The Church's teaching office cannot, even by dogmatic definition, determine the genuine meaning of Sacred Scripture."[18]

As recently as the International Theological Commission's brief but seminal work *The Interpretation of Theological Truths* (1988) Rome has continued to affirm that any conflict between exegesis and dogma is provoked by unfaithful exegesis. Genuinely Catholic exegesis will, by definition, always seek and find the appropriate harmony between biblical text and ecclesiastical dogma. In this light, the Pontifical Biblical Commission comments:

> False paths [i.e., in exegesis] will be avoided if actualization of the biblical message begins with a correct interpretation of the text and continues within the stream of the living Tradition, under the guidance of the Church's Magisterium.[19]

The circle of reasoning here appears to be "vicious."

In the nineteenth century the Magisterium rightly recognised that the rise of Higher Criticism and of theological Modernism would endanger the faith of Catholics (as it had already done among Protestants). But Rome faced an additional problem. The view that Sacred Tradition is also Revelation implies that the Tradition possesses the attributes of Revelation, including infallibility and inerrancy. Conse-

quently the Tradition had to be regarded as infallible. The inevitable correlate of this emerged
in Vatican I's Dogmatic Constitution *Pastor
Aeternus* in which papal infallibility was promulgated as a "divinely revealed dogma". The
Pope's *ex cathedra* definitions of faith were stated
to be "irreformable of themselves and not from
the consent of the Church" ("I myself am the
Tradition," commented Pius IX). The *anathema
sit* was pronounced on any who might
"contradict this our definition."

The later pronouncements of the Second
Vatican Council continued basically to affirm
what was historically regarded as the Tridentine
view of the relationship between Scripture and
Tradition reaffirmed in Vatican I's Dogmatic
Constitution on the Catholic Faith, *Dei Filius*.
Tradition, declared Vatican II,

> . . . derived from the apostles, develops in
> the Church with the help of the Holy
> Spirit . . . The words of the holy fathers
> witness to the presence of this living
> tradition . . . Through the same tradition
> the Church's full canon of the sacred books
> is known. . . . [20]

Especially significant is the statement made
on the relationship between Tradition and

Scripture. It employed the phraseology of Trent, apparently on papal insistence (presumably in view of the need to hold together the traditionalist and the progressive wings of the Church):

> Hence there exists a close connection and communication between Sacred Tradition and Sacred Scripture. For both of them, flowing from the same divine wellspring, in a certain way merge into unity and tend toward the same end. For Sacred Scripture is the Word of God, while Sacred Tradition takes the Word of God entrusted by Christ the Lord and the Holy Spirit to the Apostles, and hands it on to their successors in its full purity. Consequently it is not from Sacred Scripture alone that the Church draws her certainty about everything which has been revealed. Therefore both Sacred Tradition and Sacred Scripture are to be accepted and venerated with the same sense of loyalty and reverence. Sacred Tradition and Sacred Scripture form one sacred deposit of the Word of God, committed to the Church. . . .

> It is clear, therefore, that Sacred Tradition, Sacred Scripture and the teaching authority of the Church, in accord with God's most wise design, are so linked and joined together that one cannot stand without the others, and that all together and each in its

> own way, under the action of the one Holy
> Spirit, contribute effectively to the salva-
> tion of men.[21]

We ought not to make the mistake of assuming that the Roman Catholic Church is thoroughly monolithic. As we have noted, it too has a conservative and liberal wing. Problems and disagreements arise in tracing and exegeting the Tradition as much as in exegeting the Scriptures! Thus, for example, it has become characteristic of many Roman Catholic scholars to reread the Tradition in as ecumenical a fashion as possible.

One of the most interesting developments within this context has been the emergence of a school of thought especially stimulated by the work of the Tübingen theologian J. R. Geiselmann. This school argues that the view that Scripture and Tradition are twin sources of revelation, complementing one another, is a misreading of the teaching of the Council of Trent. Geiselmann appealed to what he held to be the significant change introduced into the final text of the decree through the influence of Bishop Pietro Bertano of Fano and Angelo Bonucci, the General of the Servites. The draft for the Decree on Scripture and Tradition had stated that revealed truth was to be found partly in the books of Scripture, partly in the Traditions ("*partim in libris . . . partim in . . . traditionibus*"). But the final document spoke of this truth being in the scriptural books and in the unwritten traditions ("*In libris scriptis et sine scripto traditionibus*"). Geiselmann argued from this change that Trent did not deny that all saving truth is contained in the Scriptures. The truth of divine revelation is found not partly in Scripture while the remainder is found in the traditions (the draft formulation); it is *all* in Scripture. It is also all to be found in the tradition. It could be argued therefore that the *sola Scriptura* principle, properly understood, is consistent with Trent.[22]

In response to Geiselmann's position, however, Cardinal Ratzinger (now Prefect of the Sacred Congregation of the Doctrine of the Faith) has argued that

> as a Catholic theologian, [Geiselmann] has to hold fast to Catholic dogmas as such, but none of them is to be had *sola scriptura*, neither the great dogmas of Christian antiquity, of what was once the *consensus quinquesaecularis*, nor, even less, the new ones of 1854 and 1950. In that case, however, what sense is there in talking about the sufficiency of scripture?[23]

In a word, the deposit of the faith (*depositum*

fidei) is contained in both Scripture and Tradition, and the task of interpreting it is "entrusted to bishops in communion with the successor of Peter, the Bishop of Rome."[24]

The recent document of the Pontifical Biblical Commission, *The Interpretation of the Bible in the Church,* continues to affirm this position, if in a less polemical and dogmatic manner and in an ecumenically conscious fashion: "What characterizes Catholic exegesis is that it deliberately places itself within the living tradition of the Church."[25] In this context, however, the Commission is careful to add:

> All pre-understanding, however, brings dangers with it. As regards Catholic exegesis, the risk is that of attributing to biblical texts a meaning which they do not contain but which is the product of a later development within the tradition. The exegete must beware of such a danger.[26]

No hint of criticism is made of the fact that Sacred Tradition requires belief in dogma which is not contained in Sacred Scripture. But there is present here a hint that exegetes in the past (and still today) may read the New Testament as though it had been written in the light of the Tradition, and thus distort the teaching of

Sacred Scripture (and by implication perhaps also the function of the Tradition). Implicit in this is the recognition of the substance-gap between Sacred Scripture and Sacred Tradition.

The historic Protestant view is that this gap becomes a chasm at certain strategic points. There is an unbearable discrepancy, not merely a healthy tension, between Sacred Scripture and Sacred Tradition in many areas.

In the earlier Roman Catholic handling of Scripture, any gap between the exegesis of Scripture and the content of the Tradition was minimized. The faithful Catholic exegete should not even in private exegete Scripture in a manner contrary to the Tradition:

> Furthermore, in order to restrain petulant spirits, it [the Council] decrees, that no one, relying on his own skill, shall—in matters of faith, and of morals, pertaining to the edification of Christian doctrine— wresting the sacred Scripture to his own senses, presume to interpret the said Scripture contrary to that sense which holy mother Church—whose it is to judge the true sense and interpretation of the holy Scriptures—hath held and doth hold; or even contrary to the unanimous consent of the Fathers; even though such interpretations were never [intended] to be

at any time published. Contraveners shall
be made known by their Ordinaries, and be
punished with the penalties by law established.[27]

A wide variety of factors contributed to the
Reformation of the sixteenth century. Among the
chief was the discovery, fueled by the Renaissance spirit of *ad fontes*, that the gap between the
clear teaching of Scripture and the teaching of
the Tradition was at points so great as to involve
not merely development but contradiction.

Roman Catholic scholars such as Professor
Fitzmyer have been given the freedom to explore
what Scripture teaches. They discover themselves looking over their shoulders at the Roman
Catholic traditionalists who do not hide their
anxiety that such open distancing between
Scripture and Tradition will be the downfall of
the Church. Consequently their characteristic re-
frain is that the difference between the content of
Scripture and the content of the Tradition does
not involve contradiction but only development.

What becomes clearer than ever, however, is
that the principle of *sola Scriptura* remains a wa-
tershed. As Cardinal Ratzinger as much as admitted in his reaction to Geiselmann, there are
major Roman doctrines which are simply not
found in the Scriptures. In this sense Scripture

alone cannot be regarded as sufficient for the life of the Church.

But we must go further. There are important teachings in the Tradition which are not only additional to, but different from and contradictory to, the teaching of Sacred Scripture. These include the very doctrines which were the centerpiece of the Reformation struggle: the nature of justification; the importance of the principle of *sola fide*; the number of the sacraments; the sufficiency of the work of Christ, the effect of baptism, the presence of Christ at the Supper, the priesthood of all believers, the celibacy of the priesthood, the character and role of Mary, and much else. The more that Scripture is exegeted on its own terms the more it will become clear that in these areas Sacred Tradition does not merely *add* to Sacred Scripture, it contradicts it. And if it does, can it any longer be "sacred"?

A major development has taken place, then, in Roman Catholic interpretation of Scripture. For this we may be grateful. We should not grudgingly minimize the rediscovery of the Bible. Indeed it might help us greatly if we recalled more often than we do that responsibility for the confusion in Rome's understanding of justification rests partly on the shoulders of the great Augustine himself whom we often claim with Calvin as "wholly ours."

Having said this, however, it is now clearer
than ever (*pace* Geiselmann) that the Roman
Catholic Church cannot and will not subscribe
to *sola Scriptura*. It must deny the sole sufficiency
of the Bible. And, as the Reformers recognized,
so long as Rome appeals to two sources, or even
tributaries, of revelation, the contents of Scripture and the substance of its own Tradition, it is
inevitable that it will also withstand the message
of Scripture and of the Reformation: *sola gratia,
solo Christo, sola fide.*

---

[1] See, for example, Raymond E. Brown, *The Gospel According to John,*
Vol. 2 (Garden City, N.Y.: Anchor Press, 1966) pp. 714-717.

[2] Raymond E. Brown, *Biblical Exegesis and Church Doctrine* (New York:
Paulist Press, 1985) p.9.

[3] Cited on the dustjacket of Joseph A. Fitzmyer, *Romans* (New York,
1994).

[4] Council of Trent's *Decree on Justification,* Canon XI.. See Rev. H. J.
Schroeder, O. P. *Canons and Decrees of the Council of Trent* (Rockford,
Ill.: Tan, 1978).

[5] Fitzmyer, *Romans,* p. 138.

[6] Ibid., p. 342.

[7] Ibid., p. 343.

[8] Ibid., p. 348.

[9] Ibid., p. 348.

[10] Council of Trent's *Decree Concerning Original Sin*, Session V in Schroeder.

[11] Council of Trent's *Decree on Justification*, Session VII in Schroeder.

[12] Fitzmyer, *Romans*, p. 347

[13] J.A. Fitzmyer, *Scripture, The Soul of Theology*, p. 78

[14] The translation is Fitzmyer's.

[15] See, e.g. Douglas Moo, *Romans*, Vol. 1 (Chicago.: Moody, 1991) pp. 358-9; J. Murray, *The Epistle to the Romans*, Vol. 1 (Grand Rapids: Eerdmans, 1959) pp. 205–6, 336–362.

[16] *Catechism of the Catholic Church* (Liquori, Mo.: Liquori, 1994) p. 26, #83.

[17] *Decrees on Sacred Books and on Traditions to be Received*, 1546.

[18] J. Neuner and J. Dupois, eds., *The Christian Faith in the Doctrinal Documents of the Catholic Church*, rev. ed. (Staten Island,: Alba, 1982) p. 79.

[19] *The Interpretation of the Bible in the Church* (Boston, 1993) p. 121.

---

20 *Dogmatic Consitution on Divine Revelation,* II:8. (For an English translation of the pronouncements of Vatican II, see Walter M. Abbott, ed., *The Documents of Vatican II,* New York: Crossroad, 1966).

21 Ibid., II. [10].

22 The view Geiselmann rejects has been the view of the major Roman apologists since Trent. For a brief account see J. R. Geiselmann, "Scripture, Tradition, and the Church: An Ecumenical Problem" in D. J. Callahan, H. A. Obermann, and D. J. O'Hanlon, eds., *Christianity Divided* (London, 1962) pp. 39–72.

23 J. Ratzinger in K. Rahner and J. Ratzinger, *Revelation and Tradition,* translated from the German, *Offenbarung und Überlieferung,* by W. J. O'Hara (New York, 1966) p. 33. The references to 1854 and 1950 are to the Bull *Ineffabilis Deus* promulgating the doctrine of the Immaculate Conception (i.e., the perpetual sinlessness of the virgin Mary) and to the Apostolic Constitution *Munificentissimus Deus* which promulgated the Bodily Assumption into heaven of the virgin Mary.

24 *Catechism of the Catholic Church,* p. 27, #85.

25 *The Interpretation of the Bible in the Church,* p. 89.

26 Ibid.

27 "Decree Concerning the Edition, and the Use, of the Sacred Books," in Phillip Schaff, *The Creeds of Christendom,* Vol.2 (Grand Rapids: Baker, 1966) p. 83.

7

The Transforming Power
of Scripture

Dr. Joel R. Beeke and Rev. Ray B. Lanning

In recent decades, an endless stream of books and articles has affirmed the infallibility, inerrancy, and authority of the Holy Scriptures.[1] These doctrines are essential to the Church's confession of the truth and authority of God's Word. It is both necessary and comforting for the Christian to know and believe that all Scripture is "God-breathed," that every word of every sentence is exhaled by the living God (2 Timothy 3:16). The believer would have no authority for declaring "Thus saith the Lord" in belief and practice if God had not superintended the entire process of the composition of Scripture down to every jot and tittle (Matthew 5:18). To be trusted wholly, Scripture must be wholly true and wholly trustworthy.

Needful though such affirmations are, for many evangelicals *sola Scriptura* has become largely a polemical doctrine used to counter the threats of neoorthodoxy and liberalism. As a result, evangelicals have been preoccupied with defending their view of Scripture, frequently becoming more involved with articulating what the Word *is* rather than with what the Word *says* and *does*.

The bare affirmation of the infallibility, inerrancy, and authority of Scripture is not enough for the genuine believer. Scripture is God speaking to us, as a father speaks to his children. In Scripture God gives us His Word as both a word of truth and a word of power. As a word of truth, we can trust in and rest our all upon Scripture for time and eternity. We can also look to Scripture as the source of transforming power used by the Spirit of God to renew our minds.

As Protestants and evangelicals, we must complement the defense of the doctrine of biblical inerrancy with a positive demonstration of the transforming power of God's Word. That power must be manifested in our lives, our homes, our churches, and our communities. We need to show without pretense that though other books may inform or even reform us, only one Book can and does transform us, making us conformable to the image of Christ. Only as "living epistles of Christ" (2 Corinthians 3:3) can we hope to win "the battle for the Bible" in our day. If half the strength spent in attacking or defending the Bible would be devoted to knowing and living the Scriptures, how many more would fall under the sway of their transforming power! In this chapter we shall consider the call of God to His people to be transformed; the transforming operations of His Word; those perfections of God's Word which account for its transforming power; how the Word must be used as a means of transformation; and the fruits of transformation produced in believers by the Word.

The Call to Transformation

It is the "good, acceptable, and perfect" will of God that His people be transformed. It is the high calling of God in Christ Jesus that believers be conformed to the image of His incarnate Son (Philippians 3:14; Romans 8:28–29). This transformation or "metamorphosis" is to be accomplished by the renewing of their minds; so Paul writes in Romans 12:2: "Be not conformed to this world: but be ye transformed by the renewing of your mind, that ye may prove what is that good, and acceptable, and perfect, will of God."[2] What begins as a transformation of the mind is one day to be completed in the transformation or changing of our bodies "in a moment, in the twinkling of an eye, at the last trump: for the trumpet shall sound, and the dead shall be raised incorruptible, and we shall be changed. For this corruptible must put on incorruption, and this mortal must put on immortality" (1 Corinthians 15:52–53).

The New Testament ascribes this transformation of God's people to two great divine and supernatural agencies: the Spirit of God and the Word of God. On the one hand, the apostle Paul says plainly that believers are "changed . . . from glory to glory, even as by the Spirit of the Lord." But this happens when under the preaching of the gospel by the "ministers of the new testament" they are enabled to see God's glory revealed in Christ. "We all, with open face beholding as in a glass [i.e., a mirror or looking glass] the glory of the Lord, are changed into the same image from glory to glory, even as by the Spirit of the Lord" (2 Corinthians 3:18). Consequently, it is not simply by the Word, but by the working of the Spirit with the Word that the transformation of God's people is accomplished.

On the other hand, care must be taken lest anyone should be led to think that the Word by itself has no transforming power. It is a great blasphemy to exalt the Spirit at the expense of God's Word, for God has magnified His Word above His Name (Psalm 138:2). Rather, God transforms through a combination of these two great powers, each indispensable to the other, and both inseparably joined together, so as to accomplish all God's will upon His people. Therefore the Scriptures describe the Word as a well-formed tool for a master workman's use; a mighty weapon of war for the hand of one mighty in battle; and good seed to be sown in soil well prepared to receive it by a diligent husbandman. In each case, the one is fitted for and indispensable to the other; so it is with the Word and the Spirit. Stephen Charnock put it this way:

> No sword can cut without a hand to manage it, no engine batter without a force to drive it. The word is . . . instrumental in itself, efficacious by the Holy Ghost . . . . The Word declares Christ, and the Spirit excites the heart to accept him; the word shews his excellency, and the Spirit stirs up strong cries after him; the word declares the promises, and the Spirit helps us to plead them;...the word shews the way, and the Spirit enables to walk in it; the word is the seed of the Spirit, and the Spirit the quickener of the word; the word is the

graft, and the Spirit the engrafter; the word
is the pool of water, and the Spirit stirs it
to make it healing.[3]

The Transforming Operations of God's Word

The Word of God operates as a transforming
power in various ways. In Scripture, these are
described by the use of various similes or comparisons, such as a lamp, a hammer, a sword,
and a seed.[4]

God's Word as a Lamp

"The entrance of Thy words giveth light; it
giveth understanding unto the simple" (Psalm
119:130). And in a more personal vein: "Thy
word is a lamp unto my feet, and a light unto
my path" (Psalm 119:105). So the psalmist ex-
presses the way in which God's Word acts as a
source of spiritual illumination, understanding,
and guidance. This light is important both in
the regeneration of the sinner and in the daily
life of the believer. On the one hand, the natural
condition of fallen man is one of darkness, ignorance, and blindness (Ephesians 4:18); on the
other hand, even God's people must at times
walk in a condition of spiritual darkness in
which only the light of God's Word can afford
them any comfort or hope (Psalm 130:5–6;

Isaiah 50:10).

"Unless God's Word illumine the way," wrote Calvin, "the whole life of men is wrapped in darkness and mist, so that they cannot but miserably stray."

God's Word as a Hammer

"Is not my word like a fire, saith the LORD? and like a hammer that breaketh the rock in pieces?" (Jeremiah 23:29). There is no more ugly and dismaying aspect to the condition of fallen man than the obduracy which sin and continuing in sin produce. Scripture speaks of men hardening their hearts, their minds, their necks, and their faces, in a determined effort to present to God in body and soul the stoutest show of resistance to His will for their lives. Such is the weight and force inherent in the Word of God that one blow struck by the Spirit wielding the Word as a hammer is sufficient to break rocklike, hardened hearts in pieces. In this manner the most resistant soul may be conquered, and the strongholds of sin may be pulled down.

It must be added here that one of the most fearful of all mysteries connected with the preaching of the Word is the way in which obdurate sinners may actually be all the more hardened.[5] This is the will of God for their destruction and their greater condemnation. So it was when Moses brought the Word of the Lord to Pharaoh; and so it was when Paul preached to the Jews in the synagogue at Ephesus, and "divers were hardened, and believed not" (Acts 19:9). How unsearchable are God's judgments, and His ways past finding out!

God's Word as a Sword

In his description of the whole armor of God given in Ephesians 6, the apostle Paul lists only two offensive weapons. The one is described as "all prayer" and the other is "the sword of the Spirit, which is the word of God" (Ephesians 6: 17–18). These are the weapons of Christian warfare which Paul says "are not carnal, but mighty through God to the pulling down of strong-holds" (2 Corinthians 10:4).

Hebrews 4:12 likewise describes God's Word as something like a sword, but even more effective as a weapon, because it is "sharper than any two-edged sword." The point of comparison here is the use of the sword to thrust at and to pierce a foe with deadly effect. So the Word of God can pierce and penetrate the heart of man. It pierces so deeply, and cuts with such sharpness and accuracy, dividing asunder soul and spirit, as "joints and marrow." And in so piercing and dividing asunder, the Word of God exposes and brings under its righteous judgment "the thoughts and intents of the heart."

The experience here described is well-known among Christians. It is by no means an uncommon experience among those who hear faithful preaching of God's Word, to hear from the pulpit words which speak so accurately and so poignantly of the condition of their own heart and life that they are left feeling utterly exposed, shamed, and condemned.[6]

God's Word as a Seed

"The wages of sin is death," writes Paul in Romans 6:23. Man's spiritual condition, as a creature fallen into and existing under bondage to sin, is one of deadness in trespasses and sins (Ephesians 2:1). If he is to be delivered from such a state of death, he must be quickened or made alive. This quickening is described in Scripture as "being born again." This new birth or regeneration is the work of the Spirit (John 3:5) using the "incorruptible seed" of the Word of God (1 Peter 1:23). In a similar way, James declares that God is the Father of all Christians, saying, "Of his own will begat he us with the word of truth, that we should be a kind of firstfruits of his creatures" (1:18).

In these passages, the Word is compared to a
seed with its precious cargo of life, a great potential laid up in store, awaiting only the right
conditions for germination, growth, and the
bearing of much fruit. All of this is confirmed in
detail in our Lord's Parable of the Sower. Luke
records Him as saying explicitly, "The seed is
the word of God" (Luke 8:11). The Word is the
means by which, in Henry Scougal's phrase,
"the life of God" is planted "in the soul of man."[7]
Miraculous is the result, and many are the fruits,
when this precious seed is sown in the "good
soil" of the hearts of those "ordained to eternal
life" (Acts 13:48).

Such is the depth and extent of the transformation effected by the Word of God in the lives
of God's people. They are called out of darkness
into light. Their hardness of heart is broken and
overcome; they are brought to see and know the
depths of their own sin and misery; and they are
born again to eternal life. God's Word is exalted
as the lamp of His truth, the hammer of His
righteous wrath, the sword of His Spirit, and the
seed of life eternal.

The Perfections of God's Transforming Word

What are the particular traits or characteristics of God's Word that render it so useful a tool and so powerful a weapon in the hand of the Holy Spirit? Hebrews 4:12 and Psalm 19:7–9 address this question directly. From Hebrews 4:12, we learn that God's Word is quick and powerful. From Psalm 19:7–9, we learn that God's Word is perfect and sure; right, pure, and clean; true and righteous altogether.

God's Word Is Quick and Powerful

By "quick" is meant *living* or *imbued with life*. This life of the Word is no less than the life of God Himself, for as God is, so must His Word be. This life is also *power* or *energy*, power harnessed for work. The life of God's Word is ordered and applied to the accomplishment of His purposes: "My word . . . shall not return unto me void, but it shall accomplish that which I please, and it shall prosper in the thing whereto I sent it" (Isaiah 55:11). As living seed, God's Word has power to bring forth fruit in the lives of believers, as described in the Parable of the Sower, where "the seed is the word of God" (Luke 8:11). Because the Word of God "liveth and abideth forever" (1 Peter 1:23), its vitality and potency remain both unexhausted and undiminished through time. Believers discover with Luther that "the Bible is alive, it speaks to me; it has feet, it

runs after me; it has hands, it lays hold on me.
The Bible is not antique, or modern. It is eternal."

God's Word Is Perfect and Sure
On the one hand, God's Word is *perfectly
complete*. It is everything God intends it to be.
This is the organic perfection of the rose, and
not the mechanical perfection of, say, the internal combustion engine. The one is perfect and
complete at every stage of its unfolding; the
other is the result of much trial and error by way
of inventive effort. The unfolding history of redemption is also the unfolding history of revelation. At every point, God's Word furnished believers with all they needed for faith and life.[8]
God's Word is also *free from any imperfection*
or blemish introduced by the hand of man.
Because it is perfect, God's Word is also *sure*. As
a testimony or witness, it is true and trustworthy. God's Word is sure as a revelation of what
man is to believe concerning God, and as a rule
of what duty God requires of man.[9] As Jehovah
"changeth not" (Malachi 3:6), so His Word
stands forever sure as truth unchanging and unchangeable. "For ever, O LORD, thy word is settled in heaven" (Psalm 119:89).

God's Word Is Right, Pure, and Clean

Here is the Old Testament statement of the doctrine of biblical inerrancy. The Word is said to be *right* or *straight* because it does not deviate from perfect conformity to any just standard by which truth is measurable. The Word is *pure* as a pure light is clear and bright. Here is a lamp whose flame does not flicker, and whose rays pierce to the depths of man's darkness. The Word is *clean* because it is free from all corruption, and from anything that corrupts or defiles.

God's Word Is True and Righteous Altogether

More precisely, God's Word is *truth* (Psalm 19:9, marginal note; cf. John 17:17). It is a book of truth, with no admixture of falsehood or error. It is likewise a book of *righteousness*, through and through. It is righteous in what it demands from man as God's creature and servant, righteous in the judgment it pronounces against all ungodliness and unrighteousness of men, and righteous in the promise it holds forth of justification by faith and peace with God through our Lord Jesus Christ.

*How to Use God's Word as the Means
of Transformation*

How does the believer experience the transforming power of the Word of God? The answer
of the Reformation is by making use of the
Word in various ways as a means of grace. First
of all, by the *reading* of the Scriptures; second, by
the *preaching* of God's Word; third, by the *hearing* of God's Word; and fourth, by *singing* God's
Word, that is, by singing the Psalms.[10]

Reading God's Word

Scripture teaches us that the Word of God
must not only be read publicly in worship (Acts
15:21; 1 Timothy 4:13), but also serves as a
blessing when personally read, heard, and
obeyed. "Blessed is he that readeth, and they that
hear the words of this prophecy, and keep those
things which are written therein" (Revelation
1:3).

But how must we read? Many writers have
provided us with ample direction. One of the
most helpful early Puritan works on how to read
the Scriptures was penned by Richard Greenham (c. 1535–1594) under the title *A Profitable
Treatise, Containing a Direction for the reading and
understanding of the holy Scriptures.*[11] After estab-

lishing that the preaching and reading of God's Word are inseparably joined together by God in the work of the believer's salvation, Greenham focuses on our duty regularly and privately to read the Scriptures, gleaning support from Deuteronomy 6:6, 11:18; Nehemiah 8:8; Psalm 1:2; Acts 15:21; 2 Peter 1:19.

Waxing more practical, Greenham asserts that men sin not only when they neglect to read the Scriptures, but also "...in reading amisse: therefore the properties of reuerent and faithfull reading are to bee set downe, which are these that follow":

1. Diligence   5. Conference
2. Wisedome   6. Faith
3. Preparation   7. Practise
4. Meditation   8. Prayer[12]

Numbers one through three ought to precede reading; numbers four through seven ought to follow reading; number eight must precede, accompany, and follow reading. Here is the gist of Greenham's advice.

1. *Diligence* must be employed in reading the Scriptures more than in doing anything secular. We ought to read our Bibles with more diligence than men dig for hidden treasure. Diligence

makes rough places plain; makes the difficult, easy; makes the unsavory tasty.

2. *Wisdom* must be used in the choice of matter, order, and time. In terms of matter, the believer must not try to move from the revealed to that which is not revealed, nor spend the bulk of his time on the most difficult portions of Scripture. If the minister must accomodate his preaching of the Word to the level of his hearers, "then much more the hearers themselues must apply their owne reading to their owne capacities."[13]

In terms of order, the wise reader of Scripture will aim to be firmly grounded in all the "principall points of doctrine." Moreover, Scripture reading must follow some semblance of order rather than skipping around. Only a whole Bible will make a whole Christian.

Time must also be utilized wisely. The whole of the Sabbath should be devoted to such exercises as the reading of Scriptures, but as for other days, a portion of Scripture in the morning, at noon, and in the evening is a wise balance (Ecclesiastes 3:11). In any event, no day should pass without some reading of the Scriptures.

3. Proper *preparation* is critical. Without it, Scripture reading is seldom blessed. Such

preparation is threefold: First, we must approach Scripture with a reverential fear of God and His majesty. We must approach the Word "swift to hear, slow to speak" (James 1:19), determined like Mary to lay up God's Word in our hearts. Reverential fear is always blessed, either by having our understanding enlightened, or by some other good affections put into us.

Second, we must approach Scripture with faith in Christ, looking on Him as the Messiah, who "is the lion of the tribe of Iuda, to whom it is giuen to open the booke of God." If we come to Scripture with reverence for God and faith in Christ, will Christ Himself not open our hearts as He did the hearts of the disciples traveling to Emmaus?

Third, we must approach Scripture sincerely desirous to learn of God (Proverbs 17:16). Those who bore fruit from thirty to a hundredfold, were precisely those who received the word "in a good and honest heart" (Luke 8:15). We often do not profit from Bible-reading because we come "without a heart" for divine teaching.

4. *Meditation* after reading Scripture is as critical as preparation before reading Scripture. One can read diligently, but the reading will bear no fruit if meditation does not follow. Reading may give some breadth, but only medi-

tation and study will give depth. The difference between reading and meditation is like the difference between drifting in a boat and rowing toward a destination. "Meditation without reading is erronious, and reading without meditation is barren.... Meditation makes that which wee haue read to bee our owne. He is blessed which meditates in the law day and night" (Psalm 1)."[14]

Meditation involves our mind and understanding, as well as our heart and affections. To reach a sound and settled judgment on various truths, the mind must be brought to meditative understanding. Meditation, however, also "digests" this settled judgment, and makes it work upon our affections. If our affections do not become involved, our sound meditative understanding will whittle away. The Scriptures must be transfused through the entire texture of the soul.

5. By *conference* Greenham means godly converse with ministers or other believers. "As iron sharpeneth iron: so one friend another" (Proverbs 2:7). The godly must share together what they are gleaning from the Scriptures, not in a proud manner speaking beyond what they know, but with humility, trusting that where two or three are gathered together for spiritual con-

versation, God will be among them. Such fellowship should not be carried on in "too great a multitude," nor with a shut-door policy to others.[15]

6. Our Scripture reading must be mixed with *faith*. Faith is the key to profitable reception of the Word (Hebrews 4:2); without faith it is impossible to please God (Hebrews 11:6). To read without faith is to read in vain. Actually, all eight of these guidelines for reading Scripture should be followed in the exercise of true faith.

Moreover, through reading the Word by faith, our faith will also be refined. Our Scripture reading ought often to try our faith, not only in the generalities of our lives, but also in our particulars—especially in our afflictions. As gold is tried in the fire, so faith will abide the fire of affliction.

7. The fruit of faith must be *practice*. And practice will "bring foorth increase of faith and repentance."[16] Practice is the best way to learn; and the more we put the Word into practice in the daily obedience of faith, the more God will increase our gifts for His service and for additional practice. When the Spirit sheds light upon our conscience that we are "doing" the Word we read, we also receive the great benefit of being assured that we possess faith.

8. *Prayer* is indispensable throughout our reading of Scripture—preceding, accompanying, and following. In public reading of Scripture, it is not possible to pause and pray after each verse. In private reading, we would do well to salt Scripture constantly with short, pungent, applicable petitions suggested by the particular verses being considered. Luther wrote, "Pause at every verse of Scripture and shake, as it were, every bough of it, that if possible some fruit may drop down."

If we pray for nourishment from our physical food for every meal, how much more ought we to pray for spiritual nourishment from every Bible reading! If we do not dare touch our food and drink before we pray, how do we dare touch God's holy Book—our spiritual food and drink—without prayer?

Prayer also necessarily involves thanksgiving: "If we be bound to praise God when he hath fed our bodies, how much more when hee hath fed our soules?"[17] Let us not be fervent in asking and then cold in giving thanks. Rather, let us pray to read with godly fear and humble thanksgiving, remembering that the believer who is perfunctory in Bible reading will be perfunctory in Christian living.

If the Bible is to get into us, we must get into

it. "The Bible that is falling apart," wrote Vance Havner, "usually belongs to someone who isn't." To neglect the Word is to neglect the Lord, but those who read Scripture, in Thomas Watson's words, "as a love-letter sent to you from God," shall experience its warming and transforming power.[18]

Preaching God's Word

If Scripture is such a powerful force for the transformation of the lives of God's people, with what great diligence and zeal ought preachers to expound the inscripturated Word of God! If, by God's own appointment, the faithful preaching of the Word is the first mark of a true church and the primary means of life-giving and life-transforming grace for the people of God, what a solemn responsibility rests upon those who are called to proclaim the "unsearchable riches of Christ" revealed in these "oracles of God."[19]

But this compels a searching question: If we agree that the Bible is a miraculous, powerful, living, inerrant, authoritative book, and the very breath of Jehovah, why is there not greater evidence of its transforming power in our congregations? Why do many remain so "untransformed" and worldly in conversation and action? No doubt a large part of the answer lies in their

lack of rightly reading and hearing the Word,
together with the onslaughts of Satan, an entic-
ing world, and their own sinful hearts and
undisciplined lives. After all, when television is
watched more than the Word of God is searched
and the newspaper is read more seriously than
the Scriptures, what can one expect?

The problem of a lack of transformation,
however, lies not only in the pew. It resides also
with us as ministers when we fail to respond to
the Word "in obedience unto God, with understanding, faith, and reverence,"[20] and consequently lack the power of Word and Spirit in
our preaching. Ought we then be surprised
when the people in our pews lack transformed
lives?

For the Word of God to transform the lives of
our people, we are of course always dependent
upon the work of the Holy Spirit. But this is not
the whole answer. Church history makes clear
that the Holy Spirit honors preaching which
bears certain critical and scriptural marks. As
preachers, we have the responsibility to examine
our preaching in the light of several probing
questions:

First, am I truly preaching the Word? Paul's
command to Timothy is "Preach the Word"
(2 Timothy 4:2). The command defines the task.

Timothy is to open, explain, and apply the Holy Scriptures which he has known from childhood (2 Timothy 3:15). He is to be a *minister* or *servant* of the Word. The Scriptures must be to him what a master is to a slave: all-commanding, all-providing, all-determining.

This explains why the preaching of the Reformation was expository preaching. Dr. Martin Lloyd-Jones defined expository preaching in these words:

> A sermon should always be expository. In a sermon the theme or doctrine is something that arises out of the text and its context. So a sermon should not start with the subject as such; it should start with the Scripture which has in it a doctrine or theme. That doctrine should then be dealt with in terms of this particular setting.[21]

The minister of the Word must hold himself to this task, and serve his biblical master with single-minded devotion and concentration.

Faithfulness to the example of the apostles and the Reformers requires the preacher to devote himself to prayer as well as to the ministry of the Word (Acts 6:4). Not to preach the Word is not to preach at all. Not to pray for the Spirit to use the Word as a transforming power is to preach in vain.

Second, am I preaching the whole counsel of God?
Every preacher must bear two things in mind at
all times. First, he bears a personal responsibility for the eternal welfare of his hearers. Second,
he must one day give an account of his stewardship of God's Word. When taking leave of the
Ephesian elders, Paul could make two great
claims (Acts 20:20, 27). First, "I kept back
nothing that was profitable unto you." He had
told his hearers everything needful for their
salvation and eternal well-being. Second, "I have
not shunned to declare unto you all the counsel
of God." As a messenger, Paul had fully and
faithfully delivered the message entrusted to him
by God.

All this points to the need for system, balance, diligence, and pastoral focus in preaching.
Two devices have been employed in the
churches of the Reformation to secure these
ends. The first is *lectio continua*, or serial exposition of the Scriptures. Verse by verse, chapter by
chapter, book by book, the Scriptures are
opened, explained, and applied. This method is
as old as Ulrich Zwingli and John Calvin, and
has its precedent in the preaching of the synagogue, where preaching was tied to the systematic reading of the Law and the Prophets (Luke
4:16–21).

The other method is catechism preaching, favored especially by the Dutch Reformed. Catechism preaching is the systematic exposition of a catechism, most commonly the Heidelberg Catechism, which was divided into fifty-two portions for the fifty-two Lord's Days of the year. The Catechism is on the one hand a complete and balanced presentation of biblical doctrine, and, on the other, a heart-searching application of that doctrine to the needs of the Christian, both as sinner and as saint.

Either method has its strengths and weaknesses, but both will go far toward achieving the great ends of saying all that needs to be said, from the hearers' point of view, and saying all that God would have us say as His counsel, delivered unto men and sent forth into all the world.

In any case, this whole counsel necessitates preaching unabashedly the utterly devastating analysis of the human condition that Scripture presents (Genesis 6:5; Ephesians 2:1). It necessitates preaching divine, sovereign grace as the all-sufficient, victorious answer to man's plight (Ephesians 2:5; Romans 9:16). It necessitates hemming the sinner in to this grace, calling him to faith and repentance, and offering hope exclusively in Jesus Christ for "wisdom, righteousness, sanctification, and redemption" (1 Corinthians 1:30). It necessitates preaching that the Christian must present himself "a living sacrifice of thankfulness" unto Christ (Romans 12:1).[22] It necessitates thrusting Scripture's unchangeable directives and broad-sweeping demands into every sphere of life, rather than following the kaleidoscopic agenda of men. As Luther said, rather than preaching against straw men, the faithful preacher will bring the Word of God to bear on every pertinent truth which he knows his congregation (with its peculiar temptations) needs to have addressed.

Third, am I preaching the Word of God with clarity and passion? Dr. Martin Lloyd-Jones defined preaching as "Logic on fire!"

> What is preaching? Logic on fire! Eloquent reason! Are these contradictions? Of course they are not. Reason concerning this Truth ought to be mightily eloquent, as you see it in the case of the Apostle Paul and others. It is theology on fire. And a theology which does not take fire, I maintain, is a defective theology; or at least the man's understanding of it is defective. Preaching is theology coming through a man who is on fire.[23]

Every preacher must struggle with the tendencies of his own personality. Some tend to be intellectually oriented, and their preaching is orderly, substantial, and yet quite dispassionate and cold. Others are emotionally oriented, and tend to "go for the gut." The aim of every preacher ought to be a thoroughgoing blend of order and passion, logic and fire.

It is the teaching of Scripture that we are saved "through sanctification of the Spirit and *belief of the truth*" (2 Thessalonians 2:13). The gospel is "word" (*logos*), "discourse" (*rhema*), "message" (*kerygma*), and "doctrine" (*didache*). To preach the gospel in a careless, disorderly, illogical way is to deny its very character. At the same time, the preacher is dealing with matters of the greatest significance and consequence for himself and his hearers. He must know the terrors of the Lord, and preach with fear and trembling. He must be constrained by the love of Christ, and preach with love and tears (2 Corinthians 5:9–21).

Church history has borne out that the Spirit transforms lives most frequently under biblical preaching which is brought with compelling lucidity and heartfelt conviction. In our own land, this potent combination was the underlying secret of great, mightily used preachers like Jonathan Edwards and Samuel Davies.[24]

Fourth, am I preaching the Word of God experimentally as well as doctrinally? To preach experimentally (or experientially) is to address the vital matter of Christian experience, and in particular the way in which the Christian experiences the truth of Christian doctrine in his life. The term "experimental" comes from the Latin *experimentum*, meaning "trial," derived from the verb *experior*, meaning "try, test, prove, put to the test." The same verb can also mean "to experience, to find, or know by experience," and so gives rise to the word *experientia*, meaning "trial, experiment" and "the knowledge gained by experiment."[25] Calvin used "experiential" (*experientia*) and "experimental" (*experimentum*) interchangeably, since both words, from the perspective of biblical preaching, indicate the need of "examining" or "testing" experienced knowledge by the touchstone of Scripture.[26]

Experimental preaching stresses the need to "know by experience" the great truths of the Word of God. Experimental preaching seeks to explain in terms of biblical truth, how matters *do go* and how they *ought to go* in the Christian life, and aims to apply divine truth to the whole range of the believer's experience both as an individual and in all his relationships in the family, the church, and the world around him. As

Paul Helm writes:

> The situation [today] calls for preaching
> that will cover the full range of Christian
> experience, and a developed experimental
> theology. The preaching must give guid-
> ance and instruction to Christians in terms
> of their actual experience. It must not deal
> in unrealities or treat congregations as if
> they lived in a different century or in
> wholly different circumstances. This in-
> volves taking the full measure of our mod-
> ern situation and entering with full sympa-
> thy into the actual experiences, the hopes
> and fears, of Christian people.[27]

Experimental preaching must in the first
place be discriminatory preaching. Discriminatory preaching defines the difference between the
Christian and the non-Christian. Discriminatory
preaching is the key by which the kingdom of
heaven is opened to believers and shut against
unbelievers. Discriminatory preaching promises
the forgiveness of sins and eternal life to all who
by a true faith embrace Christ as Savior and
Lord; it likewise proclaims the wrath of God and
eternal condemnation as God's judgment upon
the unbelieving, unrepentant, and uncon-verted.
Such preaching teaches us that unless our
religion be experiential, we shall perish—not

because experience itself saves, but because the Christ who saves sinners must be experienced personally as the rock upon which the house of our eternal hope is built (Matthew 7:22–27; 1 Corinthians 1:30; 2:2).

Experimental preaching is applicatory as well. It applies the text to every aspect of the hearer's life and spiritual need. In this way it seeks to promote a religion that is truly a power, and not a mere form (2 Timothy 3:5). This kind of experimental religion was defined by Robert Burns as "Christianity brought home to 'men's business and bosoms.' . . . In one word, the principle on which experimental religion rests is simply this, that Christianity should not only be known, and understood, and believed, but also felt, and enjoyed, and practically applied."[28]

How different this is from most contemporary preaching! The Word of God is often preached today in a way that will never transform anyone because it never discriminates and never applies. Preaching is then reduced to a lecture, a demonstration, a catering to the wishes and comforts of men, or a form of "experientialism" which is cut loose from the foundation of Scripture. Such preaching fails to expound from Scripture what the Reformed called *vital* religion: how a sinner is continually stripped of all his own righteousness; how he is driven to Christ alone for a full-orbed salvation; how he finds joy in simple reliance upon Christ and strives after obedience to Him, how he encounters the plague of indwelling sin, battles against backsliding, and gains the victory by faith in Christ.

It is no wonder that when God's Word is preached experimentally, it shows itself to be a great force for transformation of men and nations, as "the power of God unto salvation" (Romans 1:16). For such preaching proclaims from the gates of hell, as it were, that those who are not born again shall soon walk through these gates to eternally dwell in the homelessness of hell unless they repent (Luke 13:1–9). Such preaching proclaims from the gates of heaven that the regenerate, who by God's preserving grace persevere in holiness, shall soon walk through these gates into eternal glory and unceasing communion with the Triune God. Such preaching is transforming because it corresponds to the vital experience of the children of God (cf. Romans 5:1–11); it expounds clearly the marks and fruits of saving grace germane to the believer (Matthew 5:3–12; Galatians 5:22–23); it sets before the believer and unbeliever alike their eternal futures (Revelation 21:1–9).[29]

Fifth, does the manner of my preaching and my entire ministry confirm the message I proclaim? One of the problems of the contemporary pulpit is the jarring contrast between the serious nature of the message proclaimed and the casual and even offhand way in which it is delivered. Preachers who by their manner convey the impression that they have nothing especially important to say should not be surprised if no one gives them any serious attention.

The manner of our preaching ought to confirm the seriousness of what we have to say. The Westminster Assembly divines understood this fundamental link between style and substance. They conclude their discussion on method in preaching in *The Directory for the Public Worship of God* (1645) by taking up the matter of style or manner, and charge all preachers that both their preaching and "whole ministry" must be performed in the spirit of these seven marks: (1) *painfully*, that is, painstakingly, not negligently; (2) *plainly*, so that the most uneducated may be able to grasp the teaching of Scripture; (3) *faithfully*, yearning for the honor of Christ, the salvation of the lost, and the edification of believers; (4) *wisely*, teaching and admonishing in a manner most apt to prevail with the parishioners; (5) *gravely*, as becomes the Word; (6) *lovingly*, with godly zeal and hearty desire for the welfare of souls; (7) *earnestly*, being inwardly persuaded of the truth of Christ and walking before the flock in a godly manner, both privately and publicly.[30] If these seven qualities were exemplified more fully in today's preaching and ministry, would we not see more of the transforming power of the Word of God in the churches?

Ministers must seek grace to build the house of God with both hands—with their doctrine and their life. "Truth is in order to godliness," said the Old School Presbyterians. Doctrine must produce life, and life must adorn doctrine. Preachers must be what they preach and teach. They must not only apply themselves to their texts, but they must also apply their texts to themselves.[31] "He doth preach most," wrote John Boys, "that doth live best." Perhaps Robert Murray M'Cheyne said it best: "A minister's life is the life of his ministry.... In great measure, according to the purity and perfections of the instrument, will be the success. It is not great talents that God blesses so much as likeness to Jesus. A holy minister is an awful weapon in the hand of God."[32]

Hearing God's Word
Much of what Richard Greenham said above

about the reading of Scripture applies to the hearing of the Word as well. Thomas Watson offers specific help with regard to hearing the preaching of God's Word.[33] As we read this list, we would do well to ask after each item: *Am I really hearing the Word of God? Am I a good listener of the proclaimed gospel?*

1. When you come to God's house to hear His Word, do not forget to also prepare your soul with prayer.

2. Come with a holy appetite for the Word (1 Peter 2:2). A good appetite promotes good digestion.

3. Come with a tender, teachable heart (2 Chronicles 13:7), asking, "Lord, what wilt thou have me to do?" (Acts 9:6). It is foolish to expect a blessing if you come with a hardened, worldly-minded heart.

4. Be attentive to the Word preached. In Luke 19:48, we are told that the people "were very attentive" to Christ. Literally translated, the text says, "they hung upon him, hearing." Lydia evidenced a heart opened by the Lord when she "attended" or "turned her mind" to the things spoken by Paul (Acts 16:14). Such attentiveness also involves banishing wandering thoughts, dullness of mind, and drowsiness (Matthew 13:25). Regard the sermon as it truly is—a mat-

ter of life and death (Deuteronomy 32:47).

5. "Receive with meekness the engrafted word" (James 1:21). Meekness involves a submissive frame of heart—"a willingness to hear the counsels and reproofs of the word." Through meekness the Word gets "engrafted" into the soul and produces "the sweet fruit of righteousness."

6. Mingle the preached Word with faith: "The word preached did not profit them, not being mixed with faith" (Hebrews 4:2). "Faith," wrote Luther, "is not an achievement, it is a gift. Yet it comes only through the hearing and study of the Word." If the chief ingredient of a medicine is missing, the medicine will not be effective; so be sure not to leave out the chief ingredient, faith, as you listen to a sermon. Believe and apply the Word. Apply Christ when He is preached (Romans 13:14); apply the promises as they are spoken.

7. Strive to retain and pray over what you have heard. Don't let the sermon run through your mind like water through a sieve (Hebrews 2:1). "Our memories should be like the chest of the ark, where the law was put." As Joseph Alleine advised, "Come from your knees to the sermon, and come from the sermon to your knees."

8. Practice what you have heard. "Live out" the sermons you hear. Hearing that does not reform your life will never save your soul. Doers of the Word are the best hearers. Of what value is a mind filled with knowledge when not matched with a fruitful life?

9. Beg of God to accompany His Word with the effectual blessing of the Holy Spirit (Acts 10:44). Without the Spirit, the medicine of the Word may be swallowed, but it will not result in healing.

10. Familiarize yourself with what you have heard. When you come home, speak to your loved ones about the sermon in an edifying manner: "My tongue shall speak of thy word" (Psalm 119:172). Remember each sermon as if it will be the last you ever hear, for that may well be the case.

Under the Spirit's blessing, if these "ten commandments" for hearing the Word are conscientiously obeyed, the preached Word will be a transforming power in our lives. If, on the other hand, these directions are ignored, and the preached Word is not effectual to our salvation, it will be effectual to our condemnation. Watson rightly concludes: "The word will be effectual one way or the other; if it does not make your hearts better, it will make your chains heavier . .

. . Dreadful is their case who go loaded with sermons to hell."[34]

It should be evident from the foregoing discussion that to read, preach, and hear God's Word rightly, and so experience its transforming power, we need the help of the Holy Spirit. The Heidelberg Catechism states: "God will give His grace and Holy Spirit to those only who with hearty sighing unceasingly beg them of Him and thank Him for them."[35] *The Book of Common Prayer* (1662) offers for the second Sunday in Advent a model of such prayer for today's Christians:

> Blessed Lord, who hast caused all holy Scriptures to be written for our learning: Grant that we may in such wise hear them, read, mark, learn, and inwardly digest them, that by patience and comfort of thy holy Word, we may embrace and ever hold fast the blessed hope of everlasting life, which thou hast given us in our Saviour Jesus Christ. Amen.[36]

Singing God's Word

A fourth way in which believers experience the Word's transforming power is in the singing of the Psalms. Here is a use of God's Word neglected in our day, both in public worship and in private devotion. Former generations of God's people used the Psalms intensively. Not only were the Psalms used in public worship, both in prose and in meter, but also in family worship and in private. Christians were encouraged to memorize the metrical versions of the Psalms, so that they might praise God truly "from the heart."

This use of the Psalms has an ancient history. Although their composition and use in worship are associated especially with King David, it is clear from Scripture that at least some parts of the Psalter are much older and were used as far back as the days of Moses. One of the best known and most widely used of the Psalms bears the subtitle, "A Prayer of Moses the man of God" (see Psalm 90). The many citations from the Book of Psalms woven into the text of the New Testament remind us of the place they had in the worship and preaching of the apostolic church.

In the churches of the Reformation period, Psalm singing flourished as never before. In Calvin's view the singing of metrical Psalms served as a form of corporate or common prayer. To sing the Psalms in public worship, or at home, at work, and even on the battlefield, became the very mark of a Protestant. Though the use of other texts, both canonical and otherwise, found some place in many Reformed churches, the Psalms early achieved a place of preeminence which was not surrendered for a long time afterwards.

The reason for this is not hard to find. As Dr. Henry Beets wrote in his "Historical and Explanatory Introduction" printed with the 1927 edition of *The Psalter* used in the Christian Reformed Church at that time: "The Psalms meet the great requirements of praise, exalting God in His being and work and containing confessions of our unworthiness, our faith, our gratitude, our needs." Citing from an unidentified source, Beets adds, " 'In the Psalms we hear the abiding, eternal, fundamental note of the pious heart resounding.' "

If someone should ask why the Psalms should be used in distinction from or in preference to other hymns and songs known and used in Protestant churches today, two things must be said. First, the Psalms are God's Word, given by inspiration of the Holy Spirit. They possess an inherent life, power, and perfection which they have in common with all other parts of Holy Scripture. Secondly, it is the will of God and the command of God that His people praise Him with the Psalms (see Psalm 95:2, 98:5, 105:2; Ephesians 5:19; Colossians 3:16; James 5:13).[37]

Because the private, devotional use of the
Psalms is a form of meditating upon God's
Word, it is well that they be "hidden in the
heart" through memorization. The metrical versions of the Psalms lend themselves especially
well to this purpose. Mastery of the contents of
the Psalter will equip the believer with a rich
theology of Christian experience and a fully developed manual of praise and prayer. Christian
parents are reminded of their biblical obligation
to teach the Psalms to their children as "the
praises of the LORD" (Psalm 78:4) and "the
songs of Zion" (Psalm 137:3). Clearly the use of
God's Word in this way affords the godly family
great spiritual delight and much needed
strength and help.

It may fairly be said that the Reformation
would not have been the powerfully transforming movement that it was had it not been for
Psalm singing, which not only enriched the public and corporate worship of the churches, but
also carried the power of God's Word into the
highways and public places of the nations, and
into the homes and hearts of God's people.
Should the Holy Spirit be pleased to revive the
churches in our day, one evidence of such a revival will be a return to Spirit-filled singing of
the Psalms, both in public worship and in pri-

vate devotion.[38]

Finally, we need to ask: How may we know if the Word being read, heard, preached, and sung is really being applied to us by the Spirit of God? We may know by what precedes, accompanies, and follows that application. Prior to the Spirit's application, room is made in the soul for the Word. With the Spirit's application, there is a sense of suitability and power—be it the power of the still, small voice of the gospel (1 Kings 19:12) or the thunders of Sinai (Exodus 19:16)—which persuades us that we are receiving for the welfare of our souls precisely the word and instruction from God which we need to receive. And most importantly, when God applies His Word to our souls, "the fruits of righteousness, which are by Jesus Christ, unto the glory and praise of God" (Philippians 1:11) begin to appear. The old nature is mortified, and the sinful cult of self begins to decrease; the new nature is quickened and Christ's manifest presence in our lives increases. Where such fruit and evidence of the Spirit's working with the Word is lacking, the Word is not being used aright. "For the tree is known by his fruit" (Matthew 12:33b). What are some of the fruits or effects of the transforming power of the Word? We shall consider four: true conversion, wisdom, joy, and light for the dying.[39]

The Fruits of Transformation

True Conversion

"The law of the LORD is perfect, converting the soul" (Psalm 19:7a). Here God's Word is described as "law" or "instruction" (marginal note: "doctrine"). Under the instruction of Jehovah given in His Word, the inner life of man is changed and redirected. God's Word evokes in the heart a sincere sorrow for having provoked God by our sins, inspires a holy hatred of those sins, and awakens an urge to flee from them. At the same time, God's Word fills the heart with joy in God through Christ, and imparts a new love and delight to live according to the will of God in the obedience of faith.[40]

This is what is meant by the conversion of the soul. The character and direction of the inner life of man are revolutionized. This new direction is, however, not a new departure. Rather, it is a return to the path in which God commanded Adam to walk at the beginning. The apostle Paul describes it in these terms: "Be ye renewed in the spirit of your mind; and . . . put on the new man, which after God is created in righteousness and true holiness" (Ephesians 4:23–24). Such conversion is truly a restoration of the soul (Psalm 19:7a, marginal note).

Wisdom

A second fruit of the transforming power of God's Word is the possession of a new knowledge or spiritual wisdom concerning God. Scripture identifies sin with folly or foolishness, and there is no greater foolishness than the folly of unbelief. "The fool hath said in his heart, There is no God" (Psalm 14:1). This folly is reprehensible because it flies in the face of the evidence supplied in the "most elegant book"[41] of the creation itself. "The heaven declares the glory of God; and the firmament sheweth his handiwork" (Psalm 19:1). "For the invisible things of him from the creation of the world are clearly seen, being understood from the things that are made, even his eternal power and Godhead" (Romans 1:20). Acknowledging that some of the greatest intellectuals and philosophers of mankind have denied the existence of God, Paul declares: "Professing themselves to be wise, they became fools" (Romans 1:22).

Such folly can be conquered only by the testimony of Holy Scripture, confirmed by the witness of the Spirit in the heart. True wisdom, and life eternal, is to know God and Jesus Chirst whom He has sent (John 17:3). The folly of unbelief is banished when men receive and rest in the sure testimony of God's Word: "The testimony of the LORD is sure, making wise the simple" (Psalm 19:7b).

Joy

Modern man is plagued with unhappiness, anxiety, depression, and despair. Our age of material abundance has become a dark age of the soul, an era of spiritual poverty and dearth. The emptiness, barrenness, and ugliness of modern art, music, literature, and philosophy all bear witness to the sad plight of modern man. It is no mere coincidence that this era of cultural barrenness and degradation has been accompanied by a culture-wide abandonment of Biblical Christianity and the overthrow of the standards of conduct taught in the Word of God.

How different it is for those who hold fast to God's Word! "The statutes of the LORD are right, rejoicing the heart" (Psalm 19:8a). Statutes are standing laws, universal standards, abiding norms; God has provided His people with such laws, standards, and norms in His Word. By these we are "to regulate our life in all honesty to the glory of God, according to His will" (*Belgic*

Confession, Article 25).

Such obedience to God's law is far from burdensome to the Christian. "His commands are not grievous" (1 John 5:3b). It is rather a way of joy and rejoicing as spiritual poverty gives way to spiritual wealth. "Thy words were found, and I did eat them; and thy word was unto me the joy and rejoicing of my heart" (Jeremiah 15:16). "I have rejoiced in the way of thy testimonies, as much as in all riches" (Psalm 119:14). Thankfully there are at least some today who are turning from the lawlessness and confusion of the world of modern man, and rediscovering the joy of living a life made orderly, productive, and satisfying by the Word of God.

Light for the Dying

"The commandment of the LORD is pure, enlightening the eyes" (Psalm 19:8b). Here God's Word is characterized as *commandment*; the use of the singular at one and the same time reminds us of the divine origin, the organic unity, and the supreme authority of Holy Scripture as "the commandment of the LORD."

The words of the psalmist reveal their deepest meaning when viewed in the context of death and dying, the most fearful and universal of all the problems of human existence. As

Joseph A. Alexander wrote:

> *Enlightening the eyes* is understood by some
> of intellectual illumination with respect to
> spiritual things. But it is more agreeable to
> Hebrew usage to suppose an allusion to
> the dimness of the eyes produced by
> extreme weakness and approaching death,
> recovery from which is figuratively
> represented as an enlightening of the eye.[42]

In the face of impending death, man's wisdom fails and human authority must retreat. A dying man is left without help or comfort as the light fades and the darkness deepens around him. Modern men and women can without shame discuss fully the most intimate details of human sexuality, but lapse into embarrassed silence when the subject of death and dying is raised. Because they reject the Scriptures, the unsaved have nothing to live by and consequently have nothing to die with.

Only God's Word sheds light on these dark matters. "This God is our God for ever and ever: he will be our guide even unto death" (Ps. 48:14). If as a standing law God's Word serves us well in living our lives from day to day, it serves even better as a guide when we enter the "valley of the shadow of death" (Psalm 23:4). For those who receive God's Word as their lamp of truth, this light shines with unfaltering and unfailing brightness, a pure light revealing the secrets of the invisible world.

On the one hand we are warned of the everlasting burnings, the outer darkness, and the
worm that dies not; such is the judgment prepared for the wicked. The torment of dying is to
be prolonged into a perpetual death. On the
other, we are told of the safety, blessedness, and
rest bestowed on those who die in faith, holding
fast the promises. Best of all, we learn that "to be
absent from the body" is "to be present with the
Lord" (2 Corinthians 5:8). Only those who know
and believe by grace what God's Word reveals
can say with Paul that "to die is gain" (Philippians 1:21).

John Flavel summarized it well: "The Scriptures teach us the best way of living, the noblest
way of suffering, and the most comfortable way
of dying."

Conclusion

From the foregoing discussion we can see
why the men of the Reformation chose to rely so
exclusively on the Word of God as the sole rule
of faith and life, and to focus so intensely on the
work of preaching. In the first place they wholeheartedly received and affirmed Scripture's own

witness to itself, confirmed by the Spirit's witness in their hearts:

> We receive all these books, and these only,
> as holy and canonical, for the regulation,
> foundation, and confirmation of our faith;
> believing without doubt all of the things
> contained in them, not so much because
> the Church received and approves them as
> such, but more especially because the Holy
> Ghost witnesseth in our hearts that they
> are from God, whereof they carry the very
> evidence in themselves.
> —*Belgic Confession*, Article 5

Note the sweeping claim made for the faith of the Reformers: *They believed without doubt all things contained in Scripture.* Part of the weakness of modern evangelicalism is that for all its protests in the name of biblical inerrancy, there are too many instances in which this or that scholar calls in question some particular statement or teaching of Scripture.

In the second place, the Reformers acted on the logic of their position. They abandoned all other callings and gave themselves to preaching as the supreme work of their lives. They put a great deal into their preaching, and they expected a great deal to result from the sound preaching of the Word. Here again the modern evangelical is to be faulted, for he puts very little into his preaching by way of content or substance, on the pretext that modern man has some unique problems in hearing the Word. It is perhaps only just that he sees meager results from such preaching.

Sadly, it seems that the modern evangelical preacher is unaware of having adopted a self-defeating view of preaching, just as he is unaware of how his "evangelicalism" falls far short of the richly Biblical faith of the Reformation. As a result the evangelical churches have for some time been engaged in a search for some substitute for preaching (high church liturgics, drama, videos, jazz bands, "sacred" dance, etc.) that will win a hearing in our day. Many trials have been made of these substitutes, and though the results are uniformly unsuccessful, the desperate experiments continue, providing little more than the makings of feature articles on the religion pages of the nation's newspapers.

We don't know when this search for a substitute will cease, but the sooner it does, the better. The history of the Reformation confirms that the preaching of the Word of God is the most effective means of bringing its transforming power to bear upon the situation that confronts us in the world. What is needed is not to replace the pulpit, but to restore it. The public worship services should be purged of all the dross of things added to compete with sermonizing. The sermonizing must be purged of all the inappropriate humor, the endlessly retold and likely apocryphal stories, the pop psychology, and all the attention given to sports, politics, television, and various campaigns to reform society's ills.

When all such dross has been purged, today's preachers can return to their true calling to preach the Word in its fulness, richness, and power. They will discover that the Biblical gospel still has power to conquer unbelief and convert the lost. They will discover that the Word of God has the power to reform and revive the church. They will discover that the Word is a mighty weapon in our warfare against the world, the flesh, and the devil. In Luther's words, "The world is conquered by the Word, and by the Word the church is served and rebuilt."

They will also discover that nothing is more pleasing and acceptable to God; nothing more honored by the Holy Spirit; nothing more sure to maintain, increase, and extend the church and kingdom of our Savior, Jesus Christ; and nothing better suited to bring God's many prodigal sons and daughters back to the Father's house.

Today's Christians need to become intensely Word-centered in preaching, praying, worshiping, and living. In the words of Henry Smith:

> We should set the Word of God alway before us like a rule, and believe nothing but that which it teacheth, love nothing but that which it prescribeth, hate nothing but that which it forbiddeth, do nothing but that which it commandeth.[43]

The times await a generation of readers, preachers, and hearers who have experienced the Word of God as a transforming power in their lives.

---

[1] For an updated, annotated bibliography of these works, see Joel R. Beeke's series of articles in the *Christian Observer* from May 5 to July 7, 1995.

[2] The King James Version will be used throughout this chapter.

[3] Stephen Charnock, "A Discourse of the Word, The Instrument of Regeneration," in *The Complete Works of Stephen Charnock, B.D.* (Edinburgh: James Nichol, 1865) Vol. 3, pp. 316–17.

[4] True believers are also transformed by experiencing that the Word of God is their food to nourish them (Job 23:12), their heritage to enrich them (Psalm 23:2), their water to cleanse them (Psalm 119:9), their counselor to resolve their doubts and multiply their joys (Psalm 119:24), their fire to cause their hearts to burn with

affection (Luke 24:32), their rule to walk by (Galtians 6:16), and their mirror before which they dress as doers of the Word and not hearers only (James 1:23–25).

5 Cf. John Calvin, *Institutes of the Christian Religion*, ed. John T. McNeill and trans. Ford Lewis Battles (Philadelphia: Westminster, 1960), III, xxiv, 13-14.

6 Note that the Westminster Assembly divines called for such preaching in the churches in their day that would produce precisely these results in the hearers (see "Directory for the Public Worship of God," in *The Confession of Faith.* . . [Inverness: Publications Committee of the Free Presbyterian Church of Scotland, 1970], p. 380, for their remarks on the necessity of application in preaching).

7 Henry Scougal, *The Life of God in the Soul of Man* (Harrisonburg, Va:: Sprinkle, 1986).

8 Cf. Gerhardus Vos, *Biblical Theology* (Grand Rapids:: Eerdmans, 1948), pp. 13–17.

9 *Westminster Shorter Catechism*, Qu. 3.

10 Cf. *Westminster Confession of Faith*, XXI:5.

11 *The Works of the Reverend and Faithfvll Servant of Iesvs Christ, M. Richard Greenham*, ed. H[enry] H[olland] (London: Felix Kingston for Robert Dexter, 1599), pp. 389–97.

12 Ibid., p. 390.

13 Ibid., p. 391.

14 Ibid., p. 393.

[15] Ibid., p. 394.

[16] Ibid., p. 395.

[17] Ibid., p. 397.

[18] Many Puritans have addressed the "how-to" of Bible reading. One of the best, recently reprinted, is Thomas Watson, "How We May Read the Scriptures with Most Spiritual Profit," in *Heaven Taken by Storm: Showing the Holy Violence a Christian Is to Put Forth in the Pursuit After Glory*, ed. Joel R. Beeke (Pittsburgh: Soli Deo Gloria, 1992), appendix 2: 113–129. For a practical, twentieth-century booklet written in a Puritan vein with a helpful section on how to develop a reading plan, see Geoffrey Thomas, *Reading the Bible* (Edinburgh: Banner of Truth Trust, 1980).

[19] Cf. *Belgic Confession*, Article 29; *Heidelberg Catechism*, Question 65.

[20] *Westminster Confession of Faith*, XXI:5.

[21] Martin Lloyd-Jones, *Preaching and Preachers* (Grand Rapids: Zondervan, 1971), pp. 71–72.

[22] *Heidelberg Catechism*, Question 32.

[23] Lloyd-Jones, *Preaching and Preachers*, p. 97.

[24] *Works of Jonathan Edwards*, 2 vols. (Edinburgh: Banner of Truth Trust, 1974); *Sermons of the Rev. Samuel Davies*, 3 vols. (Morgan, PA: Soli Deo Gloria, 1993-96). Cf. Iain Murray, *Revival and Revivalism: The Making and Marring of American Evangelicalism* (Edinburgh: Banner of Truth Trust, 1994), pp. 3–31.

25 *Cassell's Latin Dictionary*, rev. ed. J. R. V. Marchant and J. F. Charles (New York: Funk & Wagnalls, n.d.).

26 Willem Balke, "The Word of God and *Experientia* according to Calvin," in *Calvinus Ecclesiae Doctor*, ed. W. H. Neuser (Kampen: Kok, 1978), pp. 20–21; cf. Calvin's *Commentary* on Zechariah 2:9.

27 Paul Helm, "Christian Experience," *Banner of Truth*, 139 (April 1975):6.

28 Robert Burns, "Introduction" in *The Works of Thomas Halyburton* (London: Thomas Tegg, 1835), pp. xiv–xv.

29 See the *Heidelberg Catechism* for a Reformed confessional statement that facilitates experimental preaching. This is evidenced by (1) the Catechism's exposition of an outline (misery, deliverance, and gratitude) that is true to the experience of believers, (2) its application of most doctrines directly to the believer's conscience and spiritual profit, and (3) its warm, personal character in which the believer is regularly addressed in the second person.

30 *The Confession of Faith*, p. 381.

31 Cf. J. A. Bengel, "Te totum applica ad textum; rem totam applica ad te" (Apply thyself wholly to the text, apply the matter of it wholly to thyself), cited in the preface of Erwin Nestle, *Novum Testamentum Graece*.

32 Andrew A. Bonar, *Memoir and Remains of Robert Murray M'Cheyne* (London: Banner of Truth Trust, 1966), p. 282.

33 The list provided here merges in summary form. Watson, *Heaven Taken by Storm*, pp. 16–18, and Thomas Watson, *A Body of Divinity*

(London: Banner of Truth Trust, 1971) pp. 377–79.

34 Ibid., p. 379.

35 *Heidelberf Catechism,* Question 116 (translation of 1934).

36 Collect for the second Sunday in Advent.

37 The New International Version inexplicably suppresses mention of the Psalms in many of these texts (cf. the KJV and other English versions). Note too that the phrase "psalms and hymns and spiritual songs," in Ephesians 5:19 and Colossians 3:16, may likely refer to the various kinds of Psalms as they are classified in the ancient Greek or Septuagint version of the Old Testament.

38 English-language Psalters are readily available. The *Genevan Psalter* of 1562 has at long last appeared in its entirety as an English version published in the *Book of Praise* used by the Canadian Reformed Churches. Various editions of the *Scottish Psalter* of 1650 are still in print, including the richly annotated edition produced by John Brown of Haddington (*The Psalms of David in Metre with Notes, Exhibiting the Connection, Explaining the Sense, and for Directing and Animating the Devotion* [Dallas, Tex.: Presbyterian Heritage, 1991]). The oldest and most widely used American version is the United Presbyterian *Psalter* published in 1912, and still reprinted today by the Heritage Netherlands Reformed Congregations, the Netherlands Reformed Congregations, and the Protestant Reformed Churches, with a substantial selection of English versions of the Genevan Psalms included. The Reformed Presbyterians ("Covenanters") have published a number of versions, the most recent of which is *The Book of Psalms for Singing.* The Associate Reformed Presbyterian Church has for many years published its version of the Psalter entitled *Bible Songs.* Most recent of American psalters is *Trinity Psalter*, published for use in the Presbyterian Church in America and

intended as a companion to *Trinity Hymnal*.

39 Additional fruits include peace (Psalm 85:8), sweetness (Psalm 119:103), freedom (John 8:31-32), and praise (Psalm 119:171).

40 Cf. *Heidelberg Catechism*, Questions 88–90.

41 *Belgic Confession,* Article 2.

42 Joseph A. Alexander, *The Psalms Translated and Explained* (Grand Rapids, Mich.: Baker, 1975) pp. 89–90.

43 Henry Smith, "Food for New-Born Babes," in *The Works of Henry Smith*, Vol. 1. (Edinburgh: James Nichol, 1866) p. 494.

Postscript

Rev. Don Kistler

The battle for the Bible has been raging since the beginning of time. Satan, the great enemy of souls, began his assault with a question: "Hath God said?" Eve, by stating that God had told her not to eat *or* touch the forbidden tree, added to what God had said; the first round went to Satan.

The slugfest goes on. Romanists add tradition to what is written in Scripture, and place it on an equal plane with Scripture. Some go even farther. Cardinal Cajetan pronounced to Martin Luther that the pope was *above* Scripture.

Many Charismatics and evangelicals place their personal experience on a par with Scripture, thereby adding to God's written revelation. We hear many tell us that "God said to me. . . ." Surely anything that God has said is authoritative and binding, so we add to Scripture in that way.

Today, subjective experience and feelings are placed on a par with Scripture. One of the venerable contributors to this volume has been ac-

cused of holding Scripture in too high an es-
teem. I have been accused of "bibliolatry" for taking a high view of Scripture. None of the contributors has come *close* to doing what God
Himself did when He declared in Psalm 138:2,
"Thou hast magnified Thy Word above all Thy
name." God has magnified His Word above His
very name; and, yes, that is indeed what the
word "above" means in the Hebrew: "over" or
"higher than."

Scripture holds a position of absolute authority in the life of the believer. That is why Paul
wrote to Titus and gave instructions in chapter 2
for men and women to follow with this as the
motive: "that the Word of God may not be dis-
honored."

Scripture is complete. God has said everything necessary for us to live the holy life to
which He calls us. Nothing further needs to be
added to what God has already revealed in His
written Word.

Properly interpreted, Scripture tells us this
truth itself. And even if there were no clear
teaching in Scripture about the sufficiency of
Scripture for all matters of faith and practice,
the very character of God would bring us to the
same conclusion. God is the all-sufficient God;
everything about Him is completely adequate.

Surely His written revelation of Himself would not be the one thing lacking in total sufficiency for His people!

When Christ was tempted He quoted the written Word, not oral tradition. In fact, most times the word "tradition" is used in Scripture, it is a critique of its being used. The usage Roman apologists normally build their case upon is in 2 Thessalonians 2:15, which John MacArthur has dealt with in his chapter on the sufficiency of the written text of Scripture.

The danger of adding to Scripture is evident, I trust. If we can add to what God has said, His Word, then why may we not add to what He has done, His redemptive work? But, then, that is exactly what Rome has done.

Sadly, modern evangelicalism is only slightly less culpable. While still professing that God's revelation in Scripture is sufficient for salvation, it has nearly, if not virtually, abandoned it in favor of modern psychological theories and techniques for sanctification. As one caller to a talk show in Pittsburgh stated, "Therapy saved my life; but God helped too!"

But the Apostle Peter has had the final word, I believe, when he wrote that "His divine power hath granted to us all things that pertain to life and godliness (*bios* as well as *zoe*), through the knowedge of Him that hath called us to glory and virtue" (2 Peter 1:3). Everything that pertains to life and godliness comes through the true knowledge of Him, which is given to us in Holy Writ. The heavens may declare the glory of God, but that knowledge can never save; that knowledge is enough to damn, but not to save. But the saving knowledge of Christ, who saves through faith alone, is given to us in the written Word of God.

Moses declared that the written revelation of God was not just idle words, but our life. May we fight for them as we would our life, for indeed they are!